G. Schirmer's Editions
of
Oratorios and Cantatas

Judas Maccabæus

An Oratorio

The Music by

G. F. Händel

Words by the
REV. THOS. MORELL, D. D.

A Special Concert Edition by
FRANK VAN DER STUCKEN

Ed. 709

G. SCHIRMER
New York/London

JUDAS MACCABÆUS

CHARACTERS REPRESENTED

Judas Maccabæus } Tenor
Israelitish Man }

Israelitish Woman, *Soprano*

Simon, the High Priest } Bass
Israelitish Messenger }

Israelitish Woman } Alto
A Priest }

Chorus: The People of Israel

ARGUMENT

Part I.—Lamentations for the death of Mattathias (the father of Judas Maccabæus and Simon), by whom the Jewish people had been roused to resist the cruelties and oppressions of Antiochus Epiphanes, the Syrian king, in his attempt to suppress their religion and liberties.—The divine favour invoked.—Judas recognized as leader.—Appeal to the patriotism of the people, and their response.—The value of liberty.—Preparations for war.—Pious trust in God, and heroic resolve to conquer or die.

Part II.—Celebration of the victories gained over the armies of Apollonius, the Governor of Samaria, and Seron, the Deputy Governor of Cœlesyria; and the valour of Judas.—Renewal of war by a division of the Syrian army from Egypt, under Gorgias, and the despondency it occasions amongst the Israelites.—Judas again arouses the failing courage of the people, and they set out to meet the enemy.—Those who remain behind utter their detestation of the Heathen Idolatries, by which the Sanctuary at Jerusalem had been desecrated, and their determination to worship only the God of Israel.

Part III.—Feast of the Dedication at Jerusalem, after Judas and his followers had recovered and restored the Sanctuary, and re-established the liberties of his country.—Return of Judas from his final victory over Nicanor and his confederates.

Part the First

No. 1. OVERTURE.

Scene.—*Modin.*

Israelites, *Men and Women, lamenting the death of* Mattathias, *Father of* Judas Maccabæus.

No. 2. CHORUS.

Mourn, ye afflicted children, the remains
Of captive Judah, mourn in solemn strains,
Your sanguine hopes of liberty give o'er;
Your hero, friend, and father is no more.

No. 3. DUET.

Israelitish Man (Tenor) and *Woman* (Soprano).

From this dread scene, these adverse pow'rs,
  Ah! whither shall we fly?
O Solyma, thy boasted tow'rs
  In smoky ruins lie!

No. 4. CHORUS.

For Sion lamentation make
With words that weep, and tears that speak.

No. 5. RECIT.—*Simon* (Bass).

Not vain is all this storm of grief;
To vent our sorrows, gives relief.

Wretched indeed! But let not Judah's race
Their ruin with desponding arms embrace.

No. 6. AIR.—*Simon.*

Pious orgies, pious airs,
Decent sorrow, decent pray'rs,
Will to the Lord ascend, and move
His pity, and regain His love.

No. 7. CHORUS.

O Father, whose Almighty pow'r
The heav'ns, and earth, and seas adore,
The hearts of Judah, Thy delight,
In one defensive band unite,
And grant a leader bold and brave,
If not to conquer, born to save.

No. 8. RECIT.—*Simon* (Bass).

I feel the Deity within,
Who, the bright Cherubim between,
His radiant glory erst display'd;
To Israel's distressful pray'r
He hath vouchsaf'd a gracious ear,
And points out Maccabæus to their aid:
Judas shall set the captive free,
And lead us on to victory.

No. 9. AIR.

Arm, arm, ye brave! a noble cause,
The cause of Heav'n, your zeal demands;
In defence of your nation, religion, and laws,
The almighty Jehovah will strengthen your hands.

CHORUS.

We come, we come, in bright array,
Judah, thy sceptre to obey!

No. 10. RECIT.—*Judas* (Tenor).

'Tis well, my friends! With transport I behold
The spirit of our fathers, famed of old
For their exploits in war.—Oh, may their fire
With active courage you, their sons, inspire!
As, when the mighty Joshua fought,
And those amazing wonders wrought,
Stood still, obedient to his voice, the sun,
Till kings he had destroy'd, and kingdoms won.

No. 11. AIR.—*Judas.*

Call forth thy pow'rs, my soul, and dare
The conflict of unequal war:
Great is the glory of the conqu'ring sword
That triumphs in sweet liberty restor'd.

CHORUS.

Lead on, lead on! Judah disdains
The galling load of hostile chains!

No. 12. RECIT.

Israelitish Woman (Soprano).

To Heav'n's almighty King we kneel,
For blessings on this exemplary zeal.
Bless him, Jehovah, bless him, and once more
To Thy own Israel liberty restore.

No. 13. AIR.

Israelitish Woman.

O Liberty, thou choicest treasure,
Seat of virtue, source of pleasure!
Life, without thee, knows no blessing,
No endearment worth caressing.

DUET (Soprano and Alto)

Come, ever-smiling liberty,
And with thee bring thy jocund train;
For thee we pant, and sigh for thee,
With whom eternal pleasures reign!

No. 14. RECIT.—*Judas* (Tenor).

My zealous father, now at rest
In the eternal mansions of the blest:
"Can ye behold," said he, "the miseries
In which the long insulted Judah lies?
Can ye behold their dire distress,
And not, at least, attempt redress?"
Then faintly, with expiring breath:
"Resolve, my sons, on liberty, or death."

We come! O see, thy sons prepare
The rough habiliments of war,
With hearts intrepid, and revengeful hands,
To execute, O Sire, thy dread commands.

No. 15. TRIO AND CHORUS.

Disdainful of danger, we'll rush on the foe,
That Thy pow'r, O Jehovah, all nations may know.

No. 16. RECIT.—*Simon* (Bass).

Haste ye, my brethren, haste ye to the field,
Dependent on the Lord, our strength and shield.

No. 17. CHORUS.

Hear us, O Lord, on Thee we call,
Resolv'd on conquest, or a glorious fall!

Part the Second.
SCENE.—*The same*.

The ISRAELITES *celebrating the return of* JUDAS *from the victories over* APOLLONIUS *and* SERON.

No. 18. CHORUS.

Fall'n is the foe: so fall Thy foes, O Lord,
Where warlike Judas wields his righteous sword.

No. 19. DUET (Soprano and Tenor) AND CHORUS.

Sion now her head shall raise,
Tune your harps to songs of praise.

No. 20. RECIT.
Israelitish Woman (Soprano).

Oh, let eternal honours crown his name,
Judas, first Worthy in the rolls of fame.
Say, "He put on the breast-plate as a giant,
And girt his warlike harness about him.
In his acts he was like a lion,
And like a lion's whelp roaring for his prey."

No. 21. AIR.—(*Israelitish Woman*).

From mighty kings he took the spoil,
And with his acts made Judah smile.

No. 22. DUET (OR CHILDREN'S CHOIR) AND CHORUS.

Hail, Judea, happy land!
Salvation prospers in his hand.

No. 23. RECIT.—*Judas* (Tenor).

Thanks to my brethren: but, look up to Heav'n!
To Heav'n let all glory and all praise be giv'n;
To Heav'n give your applause, nor add the second cause,
As once your fathers did in Midian,
Saying, "The sword of God and Gideon."
It was the Lord that for his Israel fought,
And this our wonderful salvation wrought.

No. 24. AIR.—*Judas*.

How vain is man, who boasts in fight
The valour of gigantic might,
And dreams not that a hand unseen
Directs and guides this weak machine.

No. 25. RECIT.

Israelitish Messenger (Bass).

O Judas, O my brethren!
New scenes of bloody war
In all their horrors rise.
Prepare, prepare,
Or soon we fall a sacrifice
To great Antiochus: From th'
Egyptian coast
(Where Ptolemy hath Memphis and
Pelusium lost)
He sends the valiant Gorgias, and
commands
His proud victorious bands
To root out Israel's strength, and to
erase
Ev'ry memorial of the sacred place.

No. 26. AIR AND CHORUS.

Ah! wretched, wretched Israel! fall'n
how low,
From joyous transport to desponding woe.

No. 27. RECIT.—*Judas* (Tenor).

My arms! against this Gorgias will
I go!
The Idumean governor shall know
How vain, how ineffective his design,
While rage his leader, and Jehovah
mine.

No. 28. AIR AND CHORUS.

Sound an alarm, your silver trumpets
sound,
And call the brave, and only brave,
around!
Who listeth, follow:—to the field
again!
Justice, with courage, is a thousand
men.

CHORUS.

We hear, we hear the pleasing, dreadful call,
And follow thee to conquest:—If to
fall,
For laws, religion, liberty, we fall.

No. 29. RECIT.—*Simon* (Bass).

Enough! to Heav'n we leave the
rest,
Such gen'rous ardour firing ev'ry
breast,
We may divide our cares. The field
be thine,
O Judas, and the Sanctuary mine.
For Sion, holy Sion, seat of God,
In ruinous heaps is by the heathen
trod.
Down, down with the polluted altars,
down!
Hurl Jupiter Olympius from his
throne,
Nor reverence Bacchus with his ivy
crown!
Our fathers never knew him, or his
hated crew,
Or, knowing, scorn'd such idol
vanities.

No. 30. CHORUS.

We never, never will bow down
To the rude stock, or sculptur'd stone:
We worship God, and God alone.

Part the Third.

Mount Sion.

ISRAELITISH PRIESTS, ETC., *having recovered the Sanctuary.*

No. 31. AIR.—*Priest* (Alto).

Father of Heav'n, from Thy eternal
throne
Look with an eye of blessing down,
While we prepare, with holy rites,
To solemnize the Feast of Lights.
And thus our grateful hearts employ,
And in Thy praise
This altar raise
With carols of triumphant joy.

No. 32. RECIT.

Israelitish Woman (Soprano).

O grant it, Heav'n, that our long woes may cease,
And Judah's daughters taste the calm of peace;
Sons, brothers, husbands, to bewail no more,
Tortur'd at home, or havock'd in the war.

No. 33. AIR.—*Israelitish Woman.*

So shall the lute and harp awake,
  And sprightly voice sweet descant run,
Seraphic melody to make,
  In the pure strains of Jesse's son.

No. 34. RECIT.

Israelitish Messenger (Bass).

From Capharsalama on eagle wings I fly,
With tidings of impetuous joy:
Came Lysias, with his host array'd
In coat of mail; their massy shields
Of gold and brass flash'd lightning o'er the fields;
But Judas, undismay'd,
Met, fought, and vanquish'd all the rageful train.
But lo! the conqueror comes; and on his spear,
To dissipate all fear,
He bears the vaunter's head and hand,
That threaten'd desolation to the land.

Near Jerusalem.

ISRAELITISH YOUTHS AND MAIDENS *meeting* JUDAS *on his return from the victory over* NICANOR.

No. 35. CHORUS.
(With Children's Choir.)

See, the conqu'ring hero comes!
Sound the trumpets, beat the drums;
Sports prepare, the laurel bring,
Songs of triumph to him sing.

See the godlike youth advance,
Breathe the flutes, and lead the dance;
Myrtle-wreaths and roses twine,
To deck the hero's brow divine.

No. 36. MARCH.

No. 37. CHORUS.

Sing unto God, and high affections raise
To crown this conquest with unmeasur'd praise.

No. 38. RECIT.—*Judas* (Tenor).

Sweet flow the strains, that strike my feasted ear;
Angels might stoop from Heav'n to hear
The comely songs ye sing
To Israel's Lord and King.

No. 39. AIR.—*Judas.*

No unhallow'd desire
  Our breasts shall inspire,
Nor lust of unbounded pow'r:
  But peace to obtain,
  Free peace let us gain,
And conquest shall ask no more.

No. 40. DUET.
(Soprano and Alto.)

O lovely peace, with plenty crown'd,
Come, spread thy blessings all around;
Let fleecy flocks the hills adorn,
And valleys smile with wavy corn.
Let the shrill trumpet cease, nor other sound
But nature's songsters wake the cheerful morn.

No. 41. AIR (*Simon*) AND CHORUS.
(With Children's Choir.)

Rejoice, O Judah, and in songs divine,
With cherubim and seraphim harmonious join.
Hallelujah! Amen!

INDEX

Part the First

No.			Page
1.	Overture		1
2.	Chorus	Mourn, ye afflicted children	5
3.	Duet (*Tenor* and *Soprano*)	From this dread scene	12
4.	Chorus	For Sion lamentation make	17
5.	Recitative (*Bass*)	Not vain is all this storm of grief	21
6.	Air (*Bass*)	Pious orgies, pious airs	22
7.	Chorus	O Father, whose almighty pow'r	25
8.	Recitative (*Bass*)	I feel the Deity within	32
9.	Air (*Bass*)	Arm, arm, ye brave!	34
	Chorus	We come, we come, in bright array	37
10.	Recitative (*Tenor*)	'Tis well, my friends!	41
11.	Air (*Tenor*)	Call forth thy pow'rs, my soul	42
	Chorus	Lead on, lead on!	46
12.	Recitative (*Soprano*)	To Heav'n's almighty King we kneel	50
13.	Air (*Soprano*)	O liberty, thou choicest treasure	51
	Duet (*Soprano* and *Alto*)	Come, ever-smiling liberty	53
14.	Recitative (*Tenor*)	My zealous father, now at rest	56
15.	Trio (*Alto*, *Tenor*, *Bass*) and Chorus	Disdainful of danger	58
16.	Recitative (*Bass*)	Haste ye, my brethren	65
17.	Chorus	Hear us, O Lord	65

Part the Second

18.	Chorus	Fall'n is the foe	79
19.	Duet (*Soprano* and *Tenor*) and Chorus	Sion now her head shall raise	92
20.	Recitative (*Soprano*)	Oh, let eternal honours	102
21.	Air (*Soprano*)	From mighty kings he took the spoil	103
22.	Duet (*Soprano* and *Alto*) [or Children's Choir] and Chorus	Hail, Judea, happy land	107
23.	Recitative (*Tenor*)	Thanks to my brethren!	112
24.	Air (*Tenor*)	How vain is man	113
25.	Recitative (*Bass*)	Oh Judas, oh my brethren!	119
26.	Air (*Soprano*) and Chorus	Ah! wretched, wretched Israel!	121
27.	Recitative (*Tenor*)	My arms!	128
28.	Air (*Tenor*)	Sound an alarm!	129
	Chorus	We hear, we hear the pleasing, dreadful call	134
29.	Recitative (*Bass*)	Enough! To Heav'n we leave the rest	138
30.	Chorus	We never will bow down	139

Part the Third

31.	Air (*Alto*)	Father of Heav'n!	150
32.	Recitative (*Soprano*)	Oh grant it, Heav'n	155
33.	Air (*Soprano*)	So shall the lute and harp awake	156
34.	Recitative (*Bass*)	From Capharsalama on eagle wings I fly	162
35.	Chorus [with Children's Choir]	See, the conqu'ring hero comes!	163
36.	March (*Orchestra*)		169
37.	Chorus	Sing unto God	171
38.	Recitative (*Tenor*)	Sweet flow the strains	180
39.	Air (*Tenor*)	No unhallowed desire	180
40.	Duet (*Soprano* and *Alto*)	Oh lovely peace	184
41.	Air (*Bass*)	Rejoice, oh Judah!	192
	Chorus [with Children's Choir]	Hallelujah! Amen	195

G. F. HÄNDEL

JUDAS MACCABAEUS

Part I

Rev. Thos. Morell, D.D.

A special Concert Edition by Frank van der Stucken

Nº 1. OVERTURE

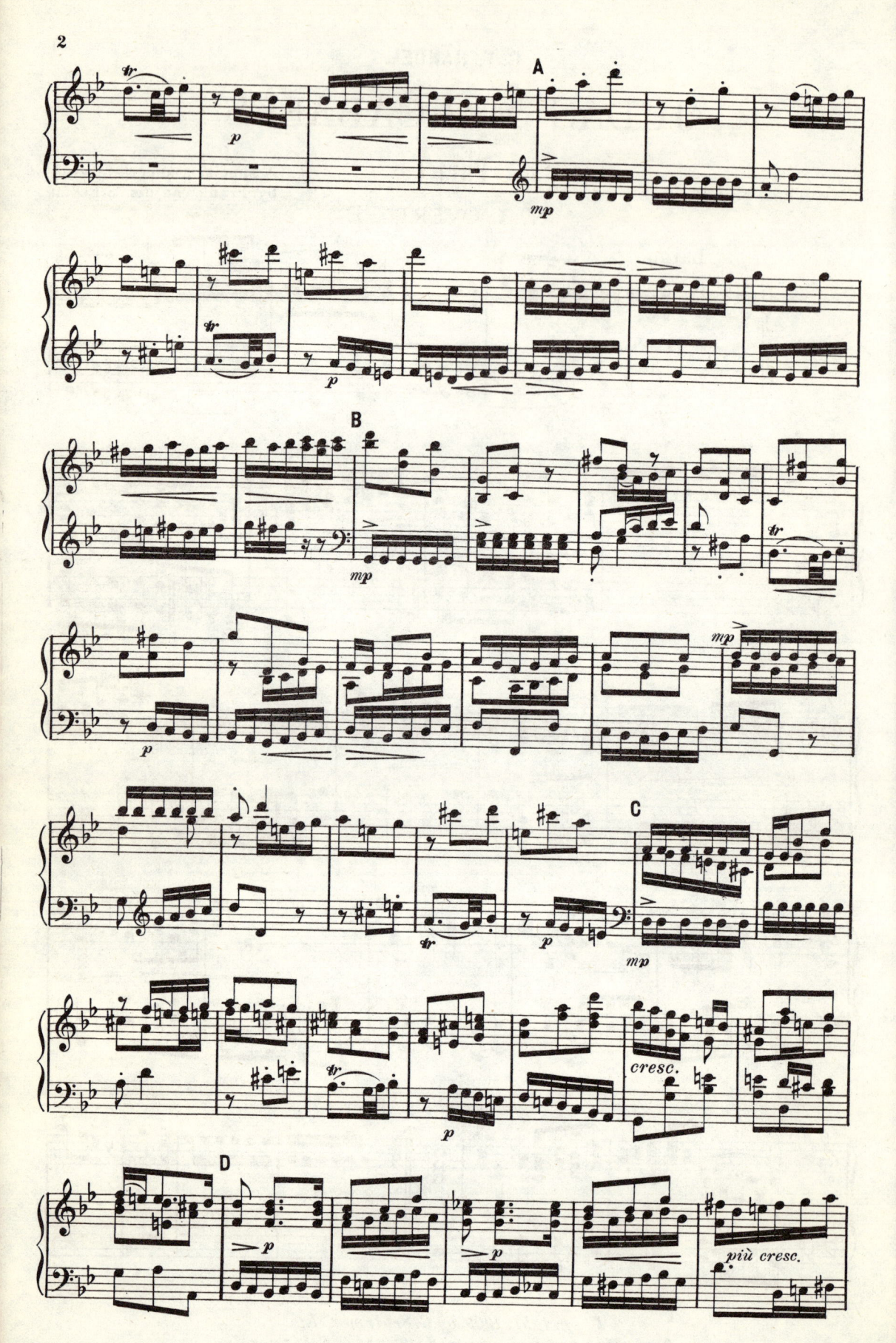
A
mp
p
B
C
D
cresc.
più cresc.

3

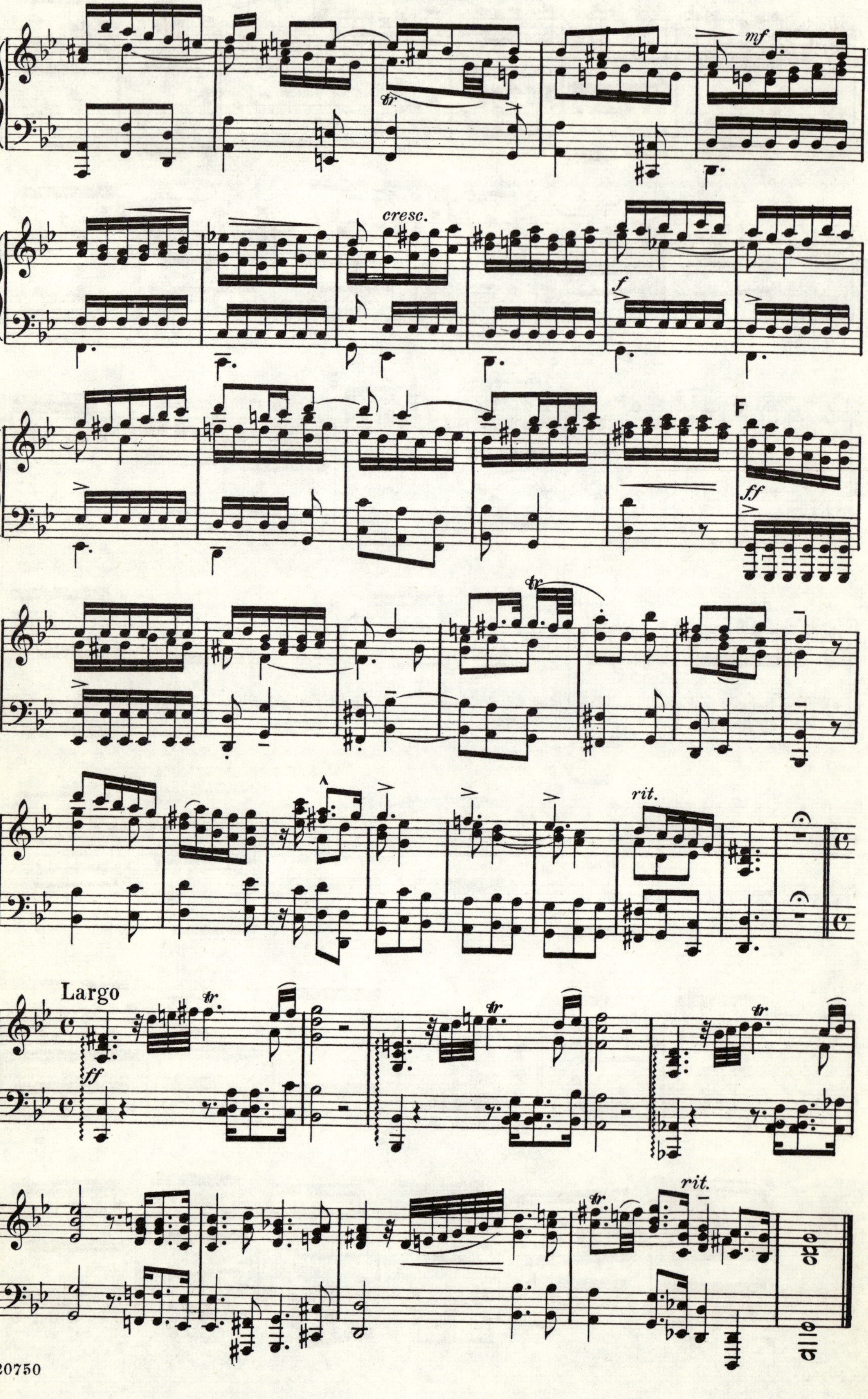
mf
cresc.
f
F
ff
rit.
Largo
ff
rit.

Nº 2. CHORUS.—"Mourn, ye afflicted children"

captive Judah, mourn in solemn strains,

Of captive Judah, mourn in solemn strains, mourn,

children, the remains Of captive Judah,

children, the remains Of captive Judah, mourn in solemn,

mourn

ye afflicted children, the remains of captive Judah, mourn in

mourn in solemn strains, Your sanguine hopes of

solemn strains, mourn, ye afflicted

in solemn strains, Your sanguine hopes of liberty give

solemn strains, mourn, mourn,

liberty give o'er, mourn,

children, mourn in solemn strains, Your sanguine hopes, your sanguine

20750

cresc.
o'er, your san-guine hopes give o'er; Your he-ro, mourn,
your hopes of lib-er-ty give o'er; Your he-ro,
your hopes of lib-er-ty give o'er; mourn, Your
hopes of lib-er-ty give o'er; Your he-ro,
A
friend, your
he-ro, your he-ro is no
friend, and fa-ther is no more,
your friend, and fa-ther is no more, mourn,
fa-ther is no more, is no more,
more, your friend and fa-ther is no
is no more, your fa-ther is no

ye af-flict-ed chil-dren, mourn, in sol-emn strains,
mourn, in sol-emn strains, in sol - emn
more; mourn in sol-emn strains,
more; mourn mourn, ye af-flict-ed
cresc.
mp
B
your fa-ther is no more, your sanguine hopes of
strains, your fa-ther is no more, your sanguine hopes of
your fa-ther is no more,
chil-dren, your fa-ther is no more,
f
p
lib-er-ty give o'er, mourn,
lib-er-ty give o'er, your sanguine hopes give o'er, your he-ro, your fa-ther,
your sanguine hopes of lib-er-ty give o'er, your he-ro, your fa-ther,
your sanguine hopes of lib-er-ty give o'er, your he-ro, your fa-ther, your
mf

mp
your he-ro is no more;
mourn,
mf
your he-ro is no more;
f
mourn,
your he-ro is no more;
mourn,
he-ro is no more;
mourn,
p
cresc.
f
mourn in sol - emn strains,
mourn in sol - emn strains, mourn, ye af-flict-ed
mourn in sol - emn strains, mourn
mourn in sol - emn strains, in sol - emn
mf
mp
mourn, ye af-flict-ed chil-dren, mourn in
chil-dren, mourn in sol - emn, sol - emn strains, in
in sol - emn strains, your san-guine hopes of lib-er-ty give
strains, mourn in sol-emn
cresc.

sol - emn strains, mourn__ in sol - emn,
sol - emn, in sol - - emn strains,
o'er, mourn__ in sol - emn strains, in sol - emn,
strains, in sol - emn strains, mourn, ye af - flict - ed chil - dren, mourn in

sol - - emn strains, mourn,__ your fa - ther, your
mourn in sol - emn strains, your he - ro, your fa - ther, mourn,__ your
sol - - emn strains, your he - ro, mourn,__ your he - ro is no
sol - - emn strains, your he - ro, your fa - ther, your he - ro is no

11

he-ro is no more, your fa-ther is no more, your fa-ther
he-ro is no more, your fa-ther is no more, your fa-ther
more, your fa-ther is no more, mourn, your fa-ther
more, your fa-ther is no more, mourn, your fa-ther

is no more, mourn, your fa-ther is no more.
is no more, mourn, your fa-ther is no more.
is no more, mourn, your fa-ther is no more.
is no more, mourn, your fa-ther is no more.

№ 3. DUET.—"From this dread scene"

Andante

ISRAELITISH MAN (Tenor)

From this dread scene, these ad-verse pow'rs, Ah! whith-er shall we fly, ah! whith-er shall we fly? O

ISRAELITISH WOMAN (*Soprano*)

fly from this dread scene? O So-ly-ma,
cresc.
- - - - y ru - ins lie!
f
mf
B
mf
thy boast-ed tow'rs in smok - - - y
From this dread scene, these ad - verse pow'rs,
mp
ru - ins lie! O
Ah! whith-er shall we fly? ah! whith-er shall we fly? O So - ly-ma!

So-ly-ma, thy boast-ed tow'rs In smok-y ru-ins lie, thy boast-ed tow'rs in smok-y ruins lie! O So-ly-ma, thy boast-ed tow'rs In smoky ru-ins lie, in smok-

O So-ly-ma, thy boast-ed tow'rs In smoky ru-ins lie, in smok-y ru-ins lie! From this dread scene, these ad-verse pow'rs, Ah! whith-er shall we

poco rit.
- - - - - - y ru - ins lie! O
fly? O So - ly - ma! O
cresc.
Adagio
Meno adagio
So - ly - ma! O So - ly - ma, thy boast - ed
So - ly - ma! O So - ly - ma, thy boast - ed
Tempo I
tow'rs In smok - y ru - ins lie!
tow'rs In smok - y ru - ins lie!
rit.

Nº 4. CHORUS.—"For Sion lamentation make"

Larghetto

18

19

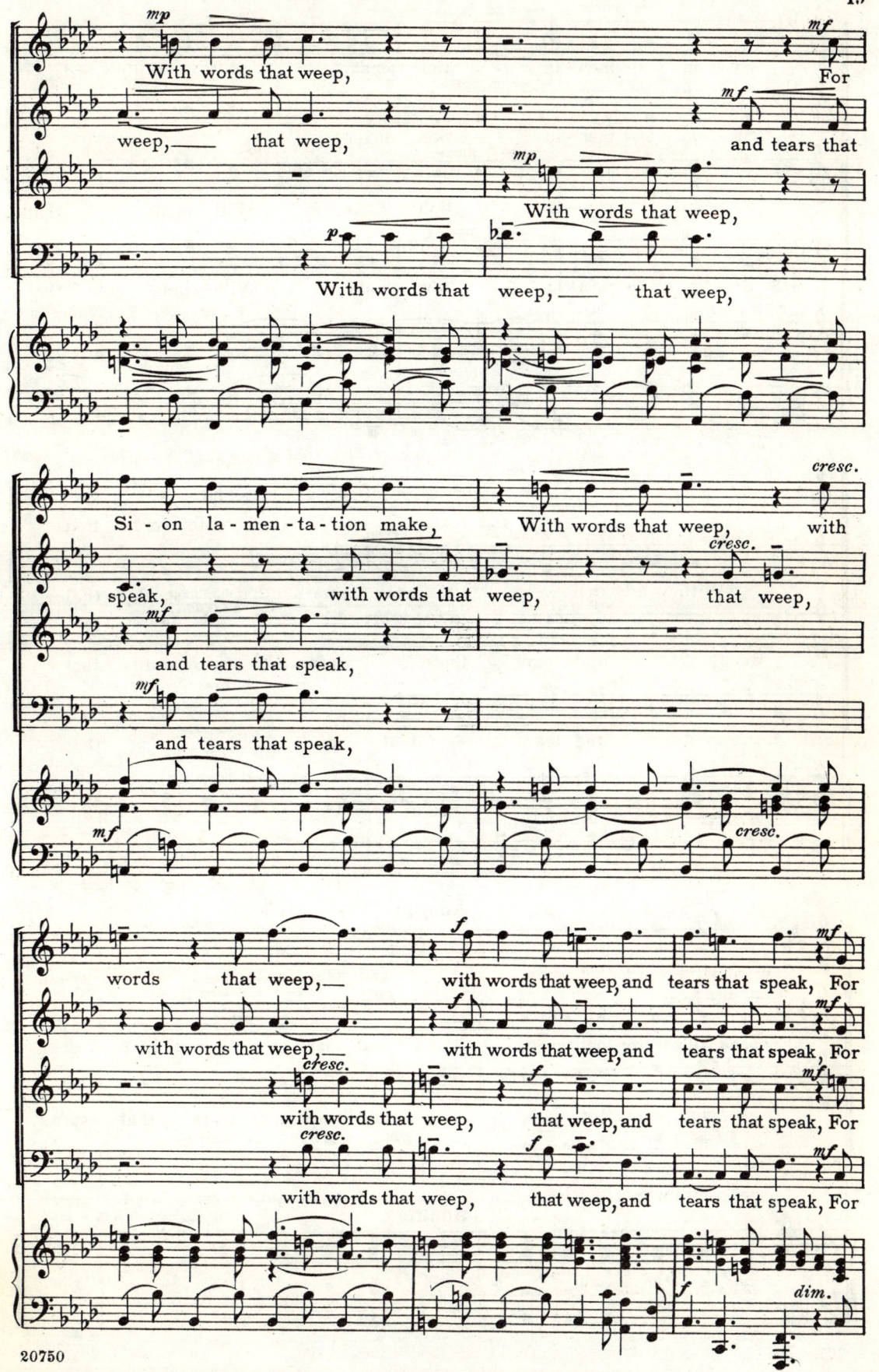

Si - on la - men - ta - tion make, With words,
Si - on la - men - ta - tion make,
Si - on la - men - ta - tion make, With words that
Si - on la - men - ta - tion make, With words that
and tears, with words that
With words that weep, and tears that speak, that
weep, and tears that speak, with words that
weep, and tears that speak, that
cresc.
Adagio
weep, with words that weep, and tears, and tears that speak.
speak, with words that weep, and tears, and tears that speak.
weep, with words that weep, and tears, and tears that speak.
speak, with words that weep, and tears, and tears that speak.
Adagio

Nº 5. RECIT. — "Not vain is all this storm of grief"

SIMON (Bass)

Not vain is all this storm of grief; To vent our sor-rows, gives re-lief. Wretch-ed in-deed! But let not Ju-dah's race Their ru-in with de-spond-ing arms em-brace.

attacca Nº 6

No 6. AIR.—"Pious orgies, pious airs"

move His pit-y, His pit-y, and re-gain His love.

Pi-ous or-gies, pi-ous airs, De-cent sor-row, de-cent sor-row, de-cent pray'rs, Will to the Lord as-cend, and move His pit-y, His pit-y, and re-gain His love. Pi-ous or-gies, pi-ous airs, De-cent sor-row, de-cent pray'rs, Will to the Lord as-cend, and move His pit-y, His pit-y, and re-gain His love.

No. 7. CHORUS.—"O Father, whose almighty pow'r"

26

seas a-dore, The
seas a-dore, The
seas a-dore, The
seas a-dore, The

hearts of Ju-dah, Thy de-light, In one de-fen-sive
hearts of Ju-dah, Thy de-light, In one de-fen-sive
hearts of Ju-dah, Thy de-light, In one de-fen-sive
hearts of Ju-dah, Thy de-light, In one de-fen-sive

band u-nite,
band u-nite,
band u-nite,
band u-nite,

20750

Allegro marcato

And grant a lead-er bold and brave, If not to con-quer, born to save; And grant a lead-er bold and con-quer, born to save, And grant a lead-er brave, If not to con-quer, born to save, And

28

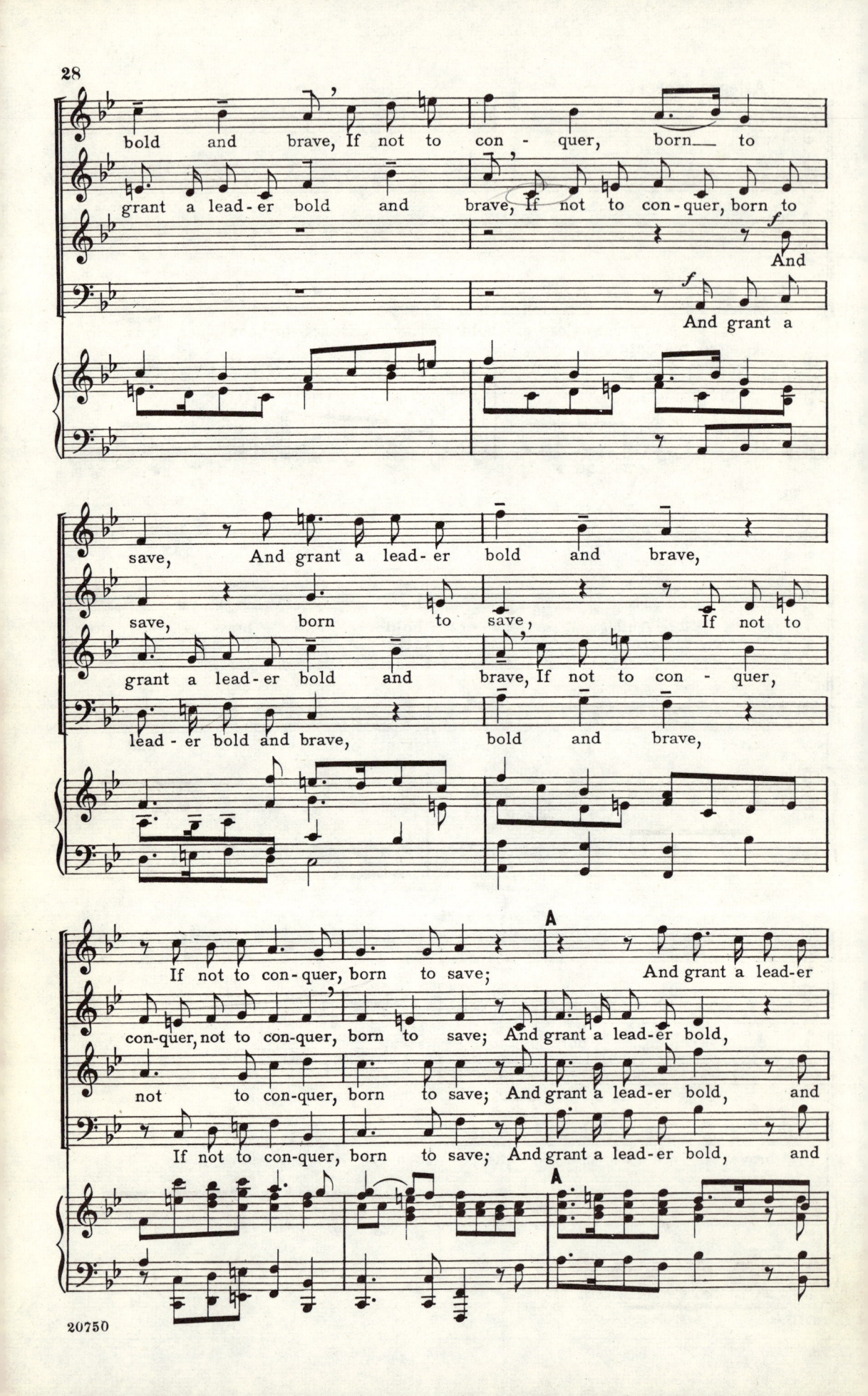

29

grant a lead-er bold and brave,
bold and brave, and grant a lead-er
bold and brave, if not to con - quer, born to
bold and brave, and grant a lead-er bold and
if not to con - quer, if
bold and brave, if not to con - quer, born to
save, and grant a lead-er
brave, if not to con - quer, born to save, and
B
not to con-quer, born to save, if not to
save, if not to con - quer, if not to
bold and brave, if not to con - quer,
grant a lead-er bold and brave, if not to con - quer,
B
f
mp

31

No 8. RECIT.—"I feel the Deity within"

Maestoso

SIMON

I feel,— I feel the Deity within, Who, the bright Cher-u-bim be-tween, His ra-diant glo-ry erst dis-play'd; To

Is-ra-el's dis-tress-ful pray'r He hath vouch-saf'd a gra-cious ear, And points out Macca-bae-us to their aid: Ju-das shall set the cap-tive free, And lead us on to vic-to-ry.

attacca No 9

Nº 9. AIR AND CHORUS.—"Arm, arm, ye brave!"

Allegro

SIMON

Arm, arm, ye brave! Arm, arm, ye brave! a no-ble cause, a no-ble cause, The cause of Heav'n, your zeal___ demands, a no-ble cause, the cause___ of Heav'n, your zeal___ demands, a no-ble cause, the cause of Heav'n, your zeal de-mands.

Arm, arm, ye brave! arm, arm, ye brave! a no-ble cause!

Arm, arm, arm, arm, ye brave! Arm, arm, arm, arm, ye brave! A

no-ble cause, the cause of Heav'n, your zeal demands, your zeal demands; Arm, arm, ye brave! A

no-ble cause, the cause of Heav'n, your zeal demands, your zeal, the cause of Heav'n your zeal demands!

In defence of your nation, religion and laws, The almighty Jehovah will strengthen your hands; In defence of your nation, religion and laws, The almighty Jehovah will strengthen, the almighty Jehovah will strengthen your hands.

Arm, arm, arm, arm, ye brave! a no - ble cause, The cause of Heav'n, your zeal demands, a no - ble cause, arm, arm, ye brave! Arm, arm, ye brave! The cause of Heav'n, your zeal de - mands!

Allegro con fuoco

CHORUS

Soprano: We come, we come, we

Alto: We come, we come, we

Tenor: We come, we come, we

Bass: We come, we come, we

20750

come, in bright ar-ray, in bright ar-ray, we come, we come, in bright ar-ray,
come, in bright ar-ray, in bright ar-ray, we come, we come, in bright ar-ray,
come, in bright ar-ray, in bright ar-ray, we come, we come, in bright ar-ray,
come, in bright ar-ray, in bright ar-ray, we come, we come, in bright ar-ray,
Ju-dah, Ju-dah, Ju-dah, Ju-dah, thy scep-tre, thy
Ju-dah, Ju-dah, Ju-dah, thy scep - tre,
Ju-dah, Ju-dah, Ju-dah, Ju - dah, thy scep-tre,
Ju-dah, Ju-dah, Ju-dah,
scep- - tre to o-bey! We
to o - bey, to o-bey! We
Ju - dah, thy scep - tre to o - bey! We
Ju - dah, thy scep - tre to o - bey! We
cresc.
mf
f

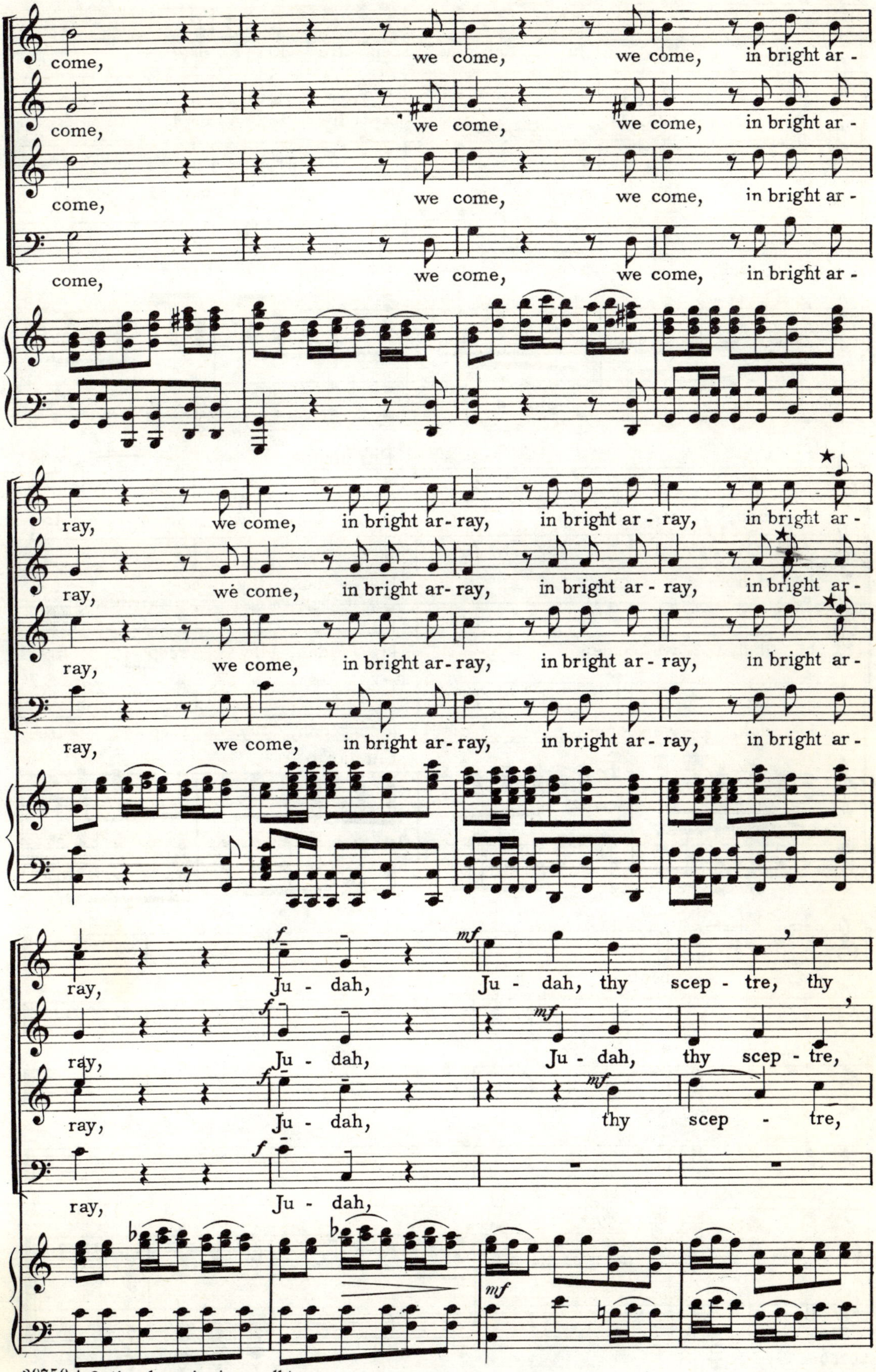

 ★Optional version in small type

sceptre, Judah, thy sceptre to obey!
Judah, thy sceptre to obey!
Judah, thy sceptre to obey!
Judah, thy sceptre to obey!

Judah, we come, Judah, thy sceptre
Judah, we come, Judah, thy sceptre
Judah, we come, Judah, thy sceptre
Judah, we come, Judah, thy sceptre

to obey!
to obey!
to obey!
to obey!

Nº 10. RECIT.—"'Tis well, my friends!"

JUDAS MACCABÆUS (*Tenor*)

'Tis well, my friends! With transport I behold The spirit of our fathers, fam'd of old For their exploits in war. Oh, may their fire With active courage you, their sons, inspire! As, when the mighty Joshua fought, And those amazing wonders wrought, Stood still, obedient to his voice, the sun, Till kings he had destroy'd, and kingdoms won.

Nº 11. AIR AND CHORUS.—"Call forth thy pow'rs, my soul"

the con-flict of un - e - qual war. Call forth thy pow'rs, my soul, and dare, and dare The con-flict of un - e - qual war, and dare the conflict of un-e-qual

war.
a tempo
Great is the
più tranquillo
glo - ry of the con - qu'ring sword, of the con - qu'ring
sword, That tri - umphs in sweet lib - er - ty re - stor'd, that
tri - - umphs in sweet lib - er - ty re - stor'd, in sweet lib - er - ty re -
Più lento
Più lento
stor'd. Call forth thy pow'rs, my soul, and dare!
a tempo

Call forth thy pow'rs, my soul, and dare!

Call forth thy pow'rs, my soul, and dare The con-flict, the con-flict of un-e- - - qual war, and dare the conflict of un-e- qual

attacca Chorus

CHORUS.—"Lead on, lead on!"

Allegro con fuoco

Soprano: Lead on, lead on, lead on!

Alto: Lead on, lead on, lead on!

JUDAS (Tenor): war. Lead on, lead on, lead on!

Bass: Lead on, lead on, lead on, lead on! Ju-dah dis-dains The gall-ing load of hos-tile chains, Ju-dah dis-dains The gall-ing

Soprano: Ju-dah dis-dains The gall-ing

Alto: Ju-dah dis-dains The gall-ing

47

48

on, lead on! Ju-dah dis-dains The gall-ing load of hos-tile, hos-tile chains, Ju-dah dis-

on, lead on! Ju-dah dis-dains The gall-ing load of hos-tile, hos-tile chains, Ju-dah dis-

on, lead on! Ju-dah dis-dains The gall-ing load of hos-tile, hos-tile chains, Ju-dah dis-

on, lead on! Ju-dah dis-dains The gall-ing load of hos - tile chains, Ju-dah dis-

dains, Ju-dah dis-dains the gall-ing load of hos - tile chains!

dains, Ju-dah dis-dains the gall-ing load of hos - tile chains!

dains, Ju-dah dis-dains the gall-ing load of hos - tile chains!

dains, Ju-dah dis-dains the gall-ing load of hos - tile chains!

No 12. RECIT.—"To Heav'n's almighty King we kneel"

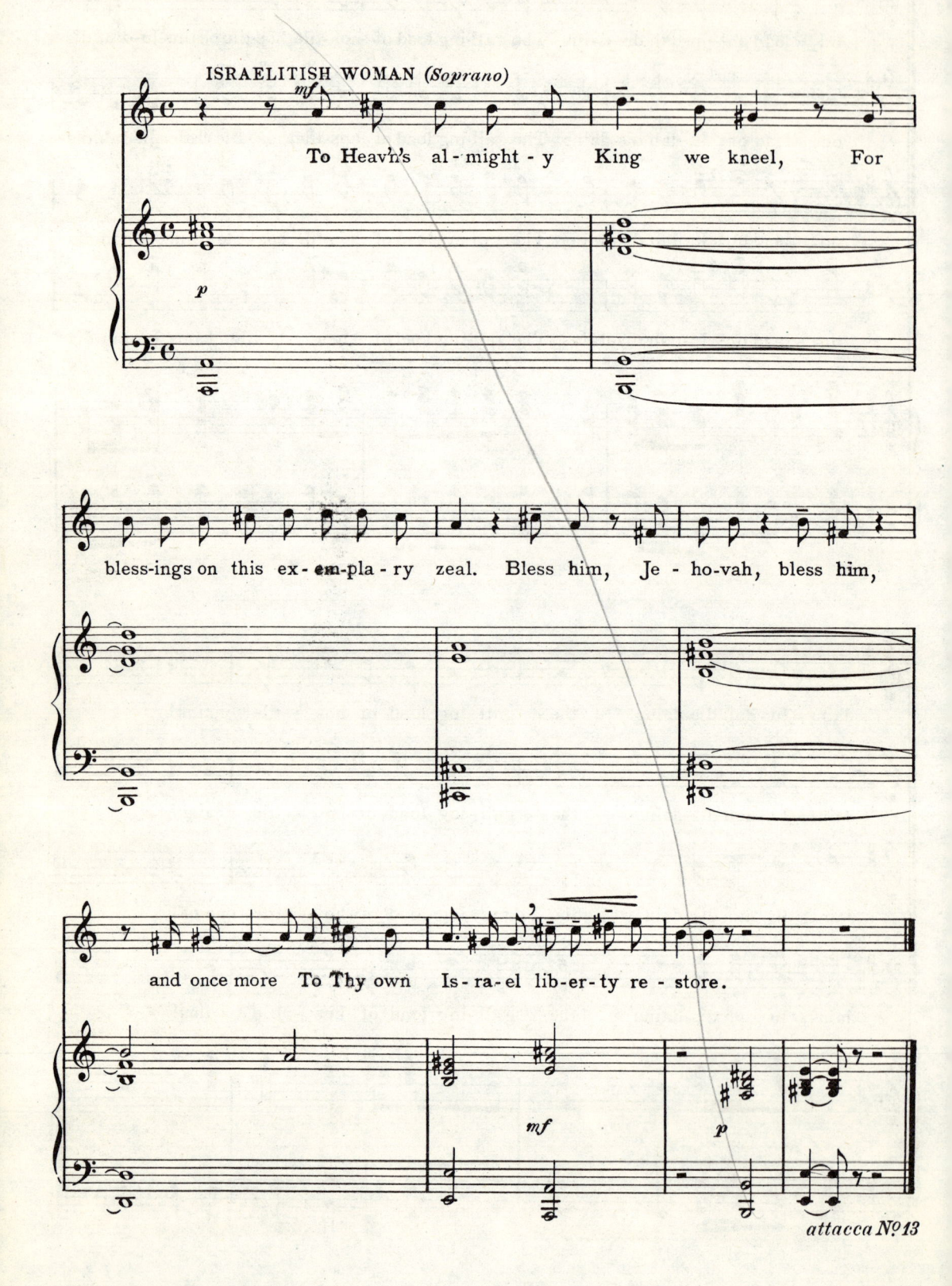

ISRAELITISH WOMAN (Soprano)

To Heav'n's al-might-y King we kneel, For blessings on this ex-em-pla-ry zeal. Bless him, Je-ho-vah, bless him, and once more To Thy own Is-ra-el lib-er-ty re-store.

attacca No 13

№ 13. AIR AND DUET
"O liberty, thou choicest treasure"

Largo sostenuto

ISRAELITISH WOMAN (*Soprano*)

O lib-er-ty, thou choicest treasure, Seat of vir-tue, source of plea-sure! Life, with-out— thee, knows no blessing, Life, with-out thee, knows no blessing, No en-dearment worth ca-ress - - ing, no endearment worth ca-ress-ing; Seat of vir-tue, source of pleasure!

O____ lib-er-ty, thou choic-est treas-ure, Seat of vir-tue, source of

pleasure! Life, without thee, knows no bless-ing, Life, without thee, knows no blessing, No en-

dear-ment, no en-dear-ment worth ca-ress - ing, no__ en-dear-ment, no en-

dear-ment worth ca-ress - ing.

Andante con moto

DUET.—"Come, ever-smiling liberty"

and with thee bring thy joc-und train;

train, with thee bring thy joc-und train;

Come, ev-er - smil-ing lib-er-ty!

Come, ev-er - smil-ing lib-er-ty!

For thee we pant, and sigh for thee, — and

For thee we pant, and sigh for thee, for thee we pant, and

sheet music

N⁰ 14. RECIT. — "My zealous father, now at rest"

JUDAS MACCABÆUS

My zeal-ous fa-ther, now at rest In the e-ter-nal man-sions of the blest: "Can ye be-hold," said he, "the mis-e-ries, In which the long-in-sult-ed Ju-dah lies? Can ye be-hold their dire dis-tress, And not, at least, at-tempt re-dress?" Then, faint-ly, with ex-pir-ing breath: "Re-solve, my sons, on lib-er-ty, or death." We come, we come! O see, thy sons pre-pare The rough ha-bil-i-ments of war, With hearts in-trep-id, and re-venge-ful hands, To ex-e-cute, O sire, thy dread com-mands.

attacca N⁰ 15

Nº 15. TRIO AND CHORUS.—"Disdainful of danger"

dain - ful of dan - ger, we'll rush on the foe, we'll
foe, on the foe, dis - dain - ful of dan - ger, we'll
we'll rush on the foe, dis - dain - ful of dan - ger, we'll
rush on the foe, dis - dain-ful of dan - ger, we'll rush on the
rush on the foe, we'll rush on the foe,
rush on the foe, dis - dain - - - - - -
foe, we'll rush on the foe, we'll rush on the foe, dis -
dis - dain - ful of dan - ger, we'll rush on the foe, dis -
- ful of dan - - - - - ger, dis -

A
mp
dain-ful we'll rush on the foe, That Thy pow'r, O Je-
mp
dain-ful we'll rush on the foe, That Thy pow'r, O Je-
mp
dain-ful we'll rush on the foe, That Thy pow'r, O Je-
f
p
cresc.
ho-vah, all na-tions may know, Thy pow'r, O Je-ho-vah, all na-tions may
cresc.
ho-vah, all na-tions may know, Thy pow'r, O Je-ho-vah, all na-tions may
cresc.
ho-vah, all na-tions may know, Thy pow'r, O Je-ho-vah, all na-tions may
know.
know.
know.
f

★ The parts in small type are additions. If they are sung, the notes in small type in the Chorus and Pianoforte parts must be considered.

62

dain-ful we'll rush on the foe,
dain-ful we'll rush on the foe,
dain-ful we'll rush on the foe,

That Thy pow'r, O Je-ho-vah, all na-tions may
That Thy pow'r, O Je-ho-vah, all na-tions may
That Thy pow'r, O Je-ho-vah, all na-tions may

know, Thy pow'r, O Je-ho-vah, all na-tions may know, That Thy
know, Thy pow'r, O Je-ho-vah, all na-tions may know, That Thy
know, Thy pow'r, O Je-ho-vah, all na-tions may know, That Thy
know, Thy pow'r, O Je-ho-vah, all na-tions may know, That Thy

64

Nº 16. RECIT.—"Haste ye, my brethren"

SIMON (Bass): Haste ye, my brethren, haste ye to the field, Dependent on the Lord, our strength and shield.

attacca Nº 17

Nº 17. CHORUS.—"Hear us, O Lord"

Andante

Soprano: Hear us, O Lord, O Lord, on Thee we

Alto: Hear us, O Lord, O Lord, hear us, O Lord,

Tenor: Hear, hear us, O Lord, O Lord,

Bass: Hear,

cresc.
call, on Thee we call, on Thee we
p
on Thee we call, O Lord,
p
on Thee we call, O Lord,
mp p cresc.
hear us, O Lord, O Lord, on Thee we call, on Thee we
call,
mf cresc. f mf mf
on Thee we call, hear us, hear us,
mf cresc. f mf mf
on Thee we call, hear us, hear us,
f f
call, hear us, hear us,
cresc.
f mf f mf
A
f
hear us, O Lord, on Thee we
f
O Lord, on Thee we call, hear us,
f
O Lord, on Thee we call, hear us,
f
hear us, O Lord, on Thee we call,
A
f

67

re - solv'd on con - quest,
re - solv'd on con - quest,
re - solv'd on con - quest, re - solv'd on
re - solv'd on con - quest, or a glo - rious,

re - solv'd on glo - rious fall, on con -
or a glo - rious fall, on con - quest,
con - quest, or a glo - rious fall, on con - quest,
a glo - rious, a glo - rious fall, a glo - rious fall,

-quest or a glo-rious fall,

on con-quest, re-solv'd on con-quest, or a glo-

on con-quest, re-solv'd on a glo-rious fall,

on con-quest, or a glo-rious fall, on

re-solv'd on con-quest, or glo-rious

-rious, glo-rious fall, a glo-rious, glo-rious

re-solv'd on con-quest, or glo-rious

con- - quest, or a glo-rious

fall, re-solv'd on con-quest,

fall, re-solv'd on con-quest, re-solv'd

fall, re-solv'd on con-quest, re-solv'd, re-solv'd on

fall, re-solv'd on con-quest, re-solv'd on con-quest,

re-solv'd on con-quest, or glo-rious fall!

on con-quest, or a glo-rious fall!

con-quest, re-solv'd on con-quest! Hear us,

on con-quest, on con-quest, or a glo-rious fall!

Poco più largo
Hear us, hear us, on Thee we call,
Hear us, hear us, O Lord, on Thee we
hear us, hear us,
Hear us, hear us, hear us, O
Poco più largo
O
call, O Lord, on Thee we call, hear us,
O Lord, on Thee we call, hear us,
Lord, O Lord, O Lord, on

Lord, on Thee we call, hear us, O Lord, on Thee we
hear us, O Lord, on Thee we
hear us, O Lord, on Thee we
Thee we call, hear us, O Lord, on Thee we

a tempo animato

call, Re-solv'd on con-quest, re-solv'd on
call, Re-solv'd on con-quest,
call, Re-solv'd on con-quest,
call, Re-solv'd on con-quest, re-solv'd on

con - quest, or a glo-rious fall, re - solv'd on con-quest, or
or a glo-rious, glo - rious fall,
or a glo - rious fall, a glo-rious
con - quest, or a glo-rious fall,
a glo - rious, glo - - - -
re - solv'd on con-quest, or a glo - rious fall, a
fall, a glo - rious, a glo - rious, glo - rious,
a glo-rious

-rious fall, re-solv'd on con-quest, or a glo-rious,
glo - rious fall, re-solv'd on con-quest, or a
glo - rious fall, re-solv'd on con-quest, or a
fall, a glo-rious fall, re-solv'd on con-quest, or a

glo - rious fall, re-solv'd on
glo - rious fall, re-solv'd on con - quest, re-solv'd on
glo - rious fall, re-solv'd on con - quest,
glo - rious fall,

con-quest, or _____ a glo - - rious fall, on con -
con-quest, or a glo - rious, glo - rious fall,
re - solv'd on
a _ glo - rious fall, a _ glo - rious fall, a glo - rious fall,

- quest, or a glo - rious fall, re - solv'd on
re - solv'd on con - quest, or glo - rious, glo - rious
con - quest, on con - quest,
re - solv'd on con - quest, or a glo - rious fall,

con-quest, or a glo - - rious, glo - -
fall, re-solv'd on con - quest, or a glo-rious
re-solv'd on con-quest, or a glo-rious fall,
re - solv'd on con - quest,

- - - - rious fall, re-solv'd on con-quest,
fall, re-solv'd on con - quest,
re-solv'd on con - quest, on con-quest,
or a glo - rious fall, re-solv'd on con-quest,

77

on con-quest, on con-quest, on con-quest, on con-quest,

on con-quest, on con-quest, on con-quest, on con-quest,

on con-quest, on con-quest, on con-quest, on con-quest,

on con-quest, on con-quest, on con-quest, on con-quest,

Andante *ff*

or a glo - rious,— glo-rious fall! Hear us, O Lord, on Thee,—

or a glo - rious,— glo-rious fall! Hear us, O Lord, on

or a glo - rious, glo-rious fall! Hear us, O Lord, on

or a glo - rious, glo-rious fall! Hear us, O Lord, on

20750

78

O Lord, on Thee we call, Resolv'd on conquest, or a glorious fall!

Thee, O Lord, on Thee we call, Resolv'd on conquest, or a glorious fall!

Thee, O Lord, on Thee we call, Resolv'd on conquest, or a glorious fall!

Thee, O Lord, on Thee we call, Resolv'd on conquest, or a glorious fall!

20750

Part II

№ 18. CHORUS._ "Fall'n is the foe"

Allegro moderato

CHORUS
Tenor
f
Fall'n is the foe, fall'n is the foe: so fall_ Thy foes, so
Bass
f
Fall'n is the foe, fall'n is the foe: so fall_ Thy foes, so
f
Soprano
f
Fall'n is the foe,
Alto
f
Fall'n is the foe:
fall Thy foes, oh Lord!
fall Thy foes, oh Lord!
so fall___ Thy foes;
Fall'n is the foe: so fall___ Thy foes,

81

wields___ his right - eous sword, where war - like Ju - das

Where war - like Ju - das

wields___ his right - eous sword, his right-eous, right -

wields___ his right - eous sword, his right-eous sword,

Where war-like Ju - das

-eous, right-eous sword, where war-like Ju - das wields his right-eous wields his right - eous sword, his right - eous,

Where war-like Ju - das wields his right - eous,

sword, his right - eous sword, his right-eous sword.

where war-like Ju - das right - eous sword, his right-eous sword, his right - eous

right - eous sword,

wields his right - - - - - - - eous
sword, where war-like Ju-das wields his right - - - - eous
where war-like Ju - das wields his right - eous
f
mf
cresc.
B
Fall'n is the foe, where war-like Ju - das
sword. Fall'n is the foe, where
sword. Fall'n is the foe:
sword. Fall'n is the foe: so
B
f

85

C
war - like Ju - das wields his right-eous sword.
Fall'n,
Fall'n is the foe, fall'n is the foe,
Fall'n,
wields his right - eous sword.
Fall'n,
sword. Fall'n is the foe,
Fall'n,
fall'n, fall'n is the foe, fall'n,
fall'n, fall'n is the foe, fall'n,
fall'n, fall'n is the foe, fall'n,
fall'n, fall'n is the foe, fall'n,
fall'n is the foe, where war-like Ju - das wields his
fall'n is the foe,
fall'n is the foe,
fall'n is the foe,

right-eous sword, where war-like Ju - das wields___ his

where war-like Ju - das wields___ his

right-eous sword, his righteous, right - - eous

right-eous sword, his righteous, right - - eous

sword, his right-eous sword.

sword, where war-like Ju - das wields his right - eous

where war-like Ju - das wields his right - eous

D

Fall'n is the foe, where war-like

where war-like Ju - das wields his

sword, his righteous sword.

sword, his righteous sword.

Ju - das wields his right - eous sword.

right - eous sword, his right - eous, right -

Fall'n is the foe, where war - like Ju - das

Fall'n is the foe, so fall Thy foes, oh Lord!

Fall'n is the foe, where war - like Ju - das,

- eous sword, where war - like Ju - das,

wields his right - eous sword, where war - like Ju - das,

Fall'n is the foe, where war - like Ju - das,

90

war-like Ju - das wields, wields, wields his right-eous sword.

war-like Ju - das wields, wields, wields his right-eous sword.

war-like Ju - das wields, wields, wields his right-eous sword.

war-like Ju - das wields, wields, wields his right-eous sword.

E
Fall'n, fall'n, fall'n is the foe: so

Fall'n, fall'n, fall'n is the foe: so

Fall'n, fall'n, fall'n is the foe: so

Fall'n, fall'n, fall'n is the foe: so

20750

91

fall Thy foes, oh Lord, so fall Thy foes, oh Lord!

fall Thy foes, oh Lord, so fall Thy foes, oh Lord!

fall Thy foes, oh Lord, so fall Thy foes, oh Lord!

fall Thy foes, oh Lord, so fall Thy foes, oh Lord!

p cresc. molto

Where war-like Ju - das wields his right - eous

p cresc. molto

Where war-like Ju - das wields his right - eous

p cresc. molto

Where war-like Ju - das wields his right - eous

p cresc. molto

Where war-like Ju - das wields his right - eous

fp cresc. molto

Più largo

sword, where war-like Ju - das wields his right - eous sword.

sword, where war-like Ju - das wields his right - eous sword.

sword, where war-like Ju - das wields his right - eous sword.

sword, where war-like Ju - das wields his right - eous sword.

Più largo

20750

No 19. DUET AND CHORUS.—"Sion now her head shall raise"

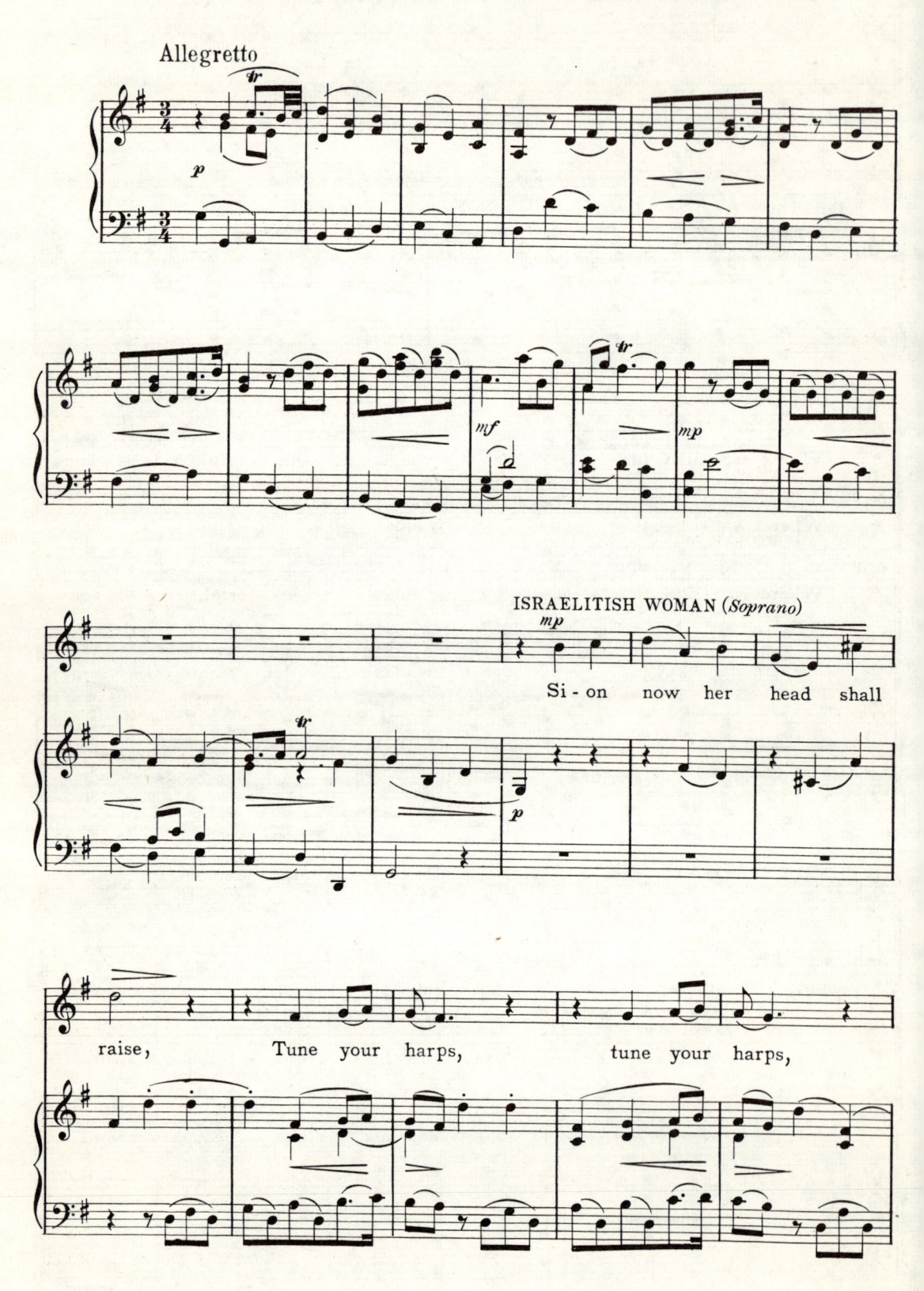

ISRAELITISH WOMAN (*Soprano*)

Si - on now her head shall raise, Tune your harps, tune your harps,

93

tune your
tune your harps to songs of praise,
harps to songs of praise, tune your harps, tune your
tune,
tune your harps, your harps, tune your
A
harps to songs of praise, tune your harps to songs of praise.
harps to songs of praise,
Sopr.
Tune your harps, tune your
Alto
Tune your harps, tune your
Tenor
Tune your harps, tune your
Bass
Tune your harps, tune your
A

harps! Si-on now her head shall raise,
harps! Si-on now her head shall raise, Tune your
harps! Si-on now her head shall raise, Tune your
harps! Si-on now her head shall raise,
Tune your harps to
harps, tune your harps, tune your harps to songs of
harps, tune your harps, tune your harps to songs of
Tune your harps to songs
songs of praise, tune your harps to songs of praise, to
praise, to songs of praise, tune your harps to songs of praise, to
praise, to songs of praise, of praise,
of praise, of praise,
f
mp
p
cresc.

songs of praise, to songs of praise, of praise.
songs of praise, to songs of praise, of praise.
tune your harps to
tune your harps to

Si-on
Si-on
songs of praise. Si-on
songs of praise. Si-on now her head shall

now her head shall raise, her head,
now her head shall raise, her head shall raise, her head shall
now her head shall
raise, her head shall raise, her head shall raise, her head shall

(Sop. I or Sop. Solo)
tune
cresc.
Si - on now her head shall raise, tune your
mf (Sop. II or Ten. Solo)
raise, now her head shall raise,
raise, her head, now her head shall raise,
raise, now her head shall raise,
your harps!
Tutti
harps, your harps, tune your harps,
tune your harps, tune your
tune, tune your
tune your harps to songs of praise,
harps, tune your harps to songs, to songs of praise, tune
harps, tune your harps to songs of praise,
harps, tune your harps to songs of praise,
cresc.
mf
mp
f
p
tr

(Sop. I or Sop. solo)
tune your
mp
mf
mf
Sop. II or Ten. Solo
tune your harps, tune your harps, tune your harps, your
your harps,
mp
tune your harps,
harps!
C
f Tutti
mp
harps, tune your harps,
mf
tune your harps, tune your harps,
mf
tune your harps, tune your harps,
f
tune, tune your harps,
C
tune your harps to songs of praise. Si - on now
f
tune your harps to songs of praise. Si - on
tune your harps to songs of praise. Si - on
tune your harps to songs of praise. Si - on
tr

99

Sop. Solo
harps!
Sop. I or Sop. Solo
Tune your harps!
mf
Sop. II or Tutti
tune your harps, your harps,
harps to songs of praise: Si-on now her
Ten. Solo mf
Tune your harps!
your harps to songs of praise:
songs of praise: Si-on now her
Sop. Solo
Tune
cresc.
your harps: Si-on now her head, now her
cresc.
head shall raise, now her
Ten. Solo
Tune
cresc.
now her head shall raise, tune your harps,
cresc.
head, now her head shall raise,

your harps!
Più largo
Tutti
head shall raise, tune your harps to songs, to of
head shall raise, tune your harps to songs, to songs of
your harps!
Tutti
tune your harps, tune your harps to songs, to songs of
tune your harps to songs, to songs of
Più largo
praise, tune your harps to songs of praise.
mf
cresc.
praise, tune your harps to songs of praise.
praise, tune your harps, your harps to songs of praise.
praise, tune your harps to songs of praise.

№ 20. RECIT. "Oh, let eternal honours"

ISRAELITISH WOMAN *(Soprano)*

Oh, let e-ter-nal hon-ours crown his name, Ju-das! first Wor-thy in the rolls of fame. Say, "He put on the breast-plate as a gi-ant, and girt his war-like harness a-bout him; in his acts he was like a li-on, and like a li-on's whelp roar-ing for his prey."

attacca № 21

No 21. AIR. "From mighty kings he took the spoil"

might - y, might - y kings he took the spoil, and
p
with his acts made Ju - dah smile, made Ju - dah smile,
p
cresc.
and with his acts made
cresc.
A
mf
Ju - dah smile. From
f

might - y kings, from might - y kings he took the spoil, And
with his acts made Ju - dah smile, and
with his acts made Ju - dah smile,
smile, smile, Ah,
and with his acts, and
f
mf
mp
p
tr

with his acts made Ju - dah smile, and with his acts made
Ju - dah smile,
cresc.
rit.
f
and with his acts made
rit.
ossia:
Ju-dah smile.
a tempo
f

Nº 22. DUET (or Children's Choir) AND CHORUS
"Hail, Judea, happy land"

Allegro marcato

(Solo, or Children's Choir)
Alto

Hail, hail, hail, Ju-de-a, hap-py land, Ju-de-a, hap-py land! Sal-va-tion pros-pers

(Solo, or Children's Choir)
Soprano

Hail, hail, hail, Ju-de-a, hap-py land, Ju-

in his hand. Ju-de-a, hap-py

de - a, hap-py land! Sal - va - tion pros - pers in his hand.
land! Sal - va - - tion prospers in his hand.
A
Sop.
Alto
Tenor
Bass
CHORUS
Hail, hail, Ju - de - a, Ju - de - a, hap - py land! Sal - va - -
Hail, hail, Ju - de - a, hap - py land, Ju - de - a, hap - py land! Sal -
Hail, hail, Ju - de - a, hap - py land, Ju - de - a, hap - py land! Sal -
Hail, hail, Ju - de - a, hap - py land, Ju - de - a, hap - py land! Sal -
- - - - tion pros - pers in his hand.
va - - tion pros - pers in his hand.
va - - - tion prospers in his hand.
va - - - tion prospers in his hand.

109

de-a, Ju-de-a, hap-py land! Sal-va - - - tion pros-pers
de-a, hap-py land, Ju-de-a, hap-py land! Sal - va - - tion pros-pers
de-a, hap-py land, Ju-de-a, hap-py land! Sal - va - tion pros - pers
de-a, hap-py land, Ju-de-a, hap-py land! Sal - va - - tion pros-pers
Soli (or Children's Choir) (ad lib.)
ff
Hail, hail, Ju-de-a! Hail, hail, Ju-
B (div. ad lib.)
ff
in his hand. Hail, hail, Ju-de-a, hap-py land, hap-py land,
in his hand. Hail, hail, Ju-de-a, hap-py land, hap-py land,
in his hand. Hail, hail, Ju-de-a, hap-py land, hap-py land,
in his hand. Hail, hail, Ju-de-a, hap-py land, hap-py land,
B
ff

de - a!
hap - py land! Sal - va - - - - - - tion
hap - py land! Sal - va - - - - - tion pros -
hap - py land! Sal - va - - - - - - - - tion
hap - py land! Sal - va - - - - - - - - tion
Più largo
a.2.
f
Sal - va - - tion pros - pers in his hand.
pros - - pers in his hand.
- pers, pros - pers in his hand.
pros - - - pers in his hand.
pros - - - pers in his hand.
Più largo

№ 23. RECIT.—"Thanks to my brethren!"

JUDAS MACCABAEUS

Thanks to my brethren! but, look up to Heav'n! To Heav'n let glory and all praise be giv'n: To Heav'n give your applause, Nor add the second cause, As once your fathers did in Midian, Saying, "The sword of God and Gideon." It was the Lord that for His Israel fought, And this our wonderful salvation wrought.

Attacca № 24

N⁰ 24. AIR.—"How vain is man"

Moderato

JUDAS MACCABAEUS

How

vain is man, who boasts in fight

The valour of gigantic might, the valour of gigantic might!

How vain is man, who boasts in fight, who

115

boasts__ in fight, who boasts__ in fight The val-our of__ gi-gan-tic might! How vain__ is man,__ who boasts__ in fight, who boasts__ in fight,__ who boasts__ in fight The val-our of gi-gan- - -tic might, the

(cut at repetition)

val-our of gi - gan - - - - - tic might!

How vain, how vain,— how vain— is man, who boasts— in fight,— who

boasts_ in fight The val-our of gi - gan - - tic might, the val-our of gi - gan - - - - - - - - - tic might, the val - - our of gi - gan-tic might! And dreams not that a hand un-seen Di-rects and guides this weak ma-chine, and dreams not that a hand un-seen di-rects and guides this weak ma-chine, di-rects and guides, di-rects and guides this weak ma-chine. How

N° 25. RECIT. "Oh Judas, oh my brethren!"

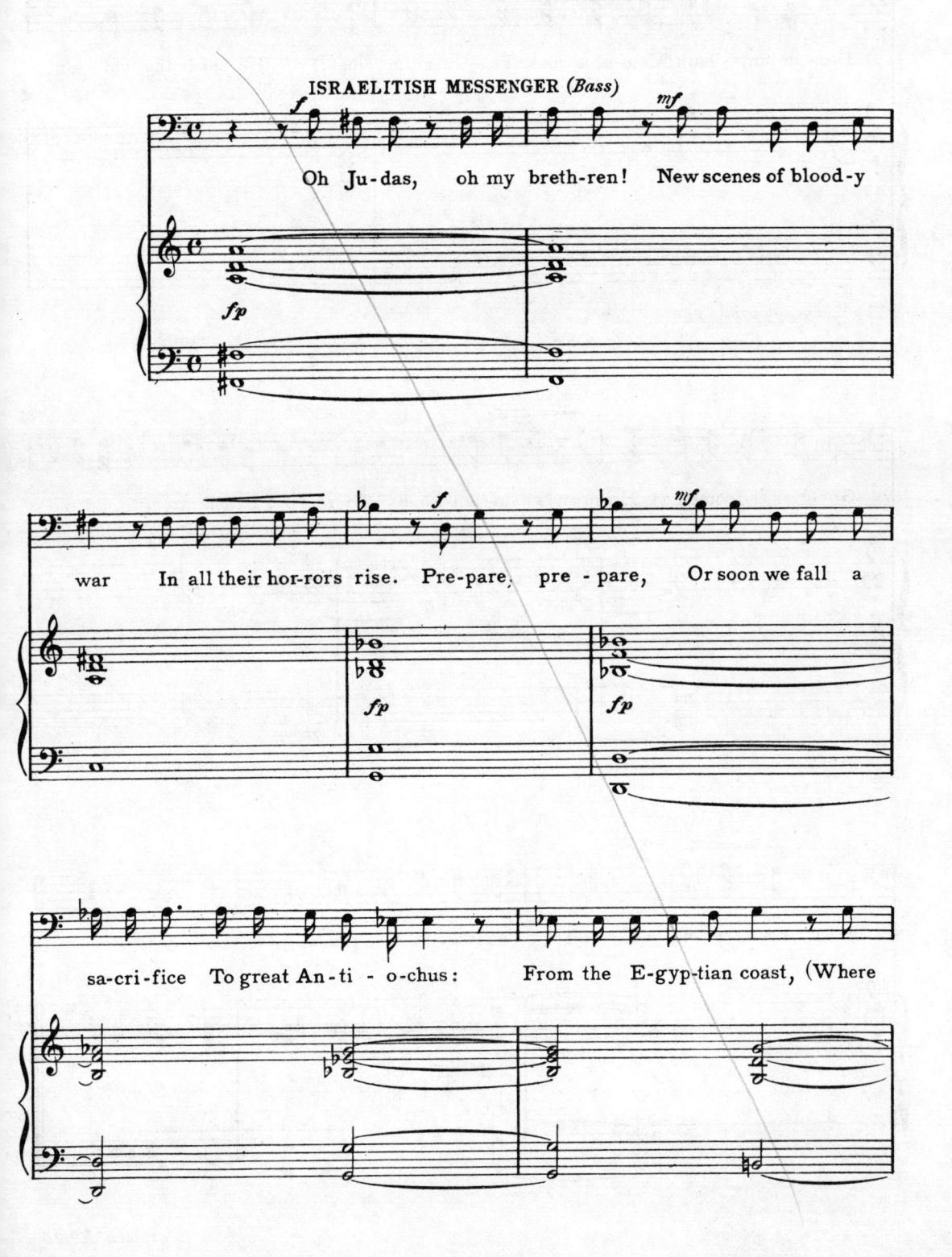

ISRAELITISH MESSENGER (Bass)

Oh Judas, oh my brethren! New scenes of bloody war In all their horrors rise. Prepare, prepare, Or soon we fall a sacrifice To great Antiochus: From the Egyptian coast, (Where

Ptolemy hath Memphis and Pelusium lost,) He sends the valiant Gorgias, and commands His proud, victorious bands To root out Israel's strength, and to erase Ev'ry memorial of the sacred place.

attacca Nº 26

No. 26. AIR AND CHORUS.— "Ah! wretched, wretched Israel!"

fall'n how low, fall'n how low,

From joy-ous trans-port, from joy-ous trans-port to despond-ing woe! Wretched Is-ra-el! wretched, wretch-ed! fall'n, fall'n from joy-ous trans-port to de-spond- -ing

A
woe!
Soprano
p
Ah! wretch - ed, wretch-ed Is - ra - el!
Alto
p
Ah! wretch-ed, wretch-ed Is - ra - el! wretch - ed Is - ra - el!
CHORUS
Tenor
p
Ah! wretch-ed, wretch-ed Is - ra - el! wretch-ed Is - ra - el!
Bass
p
Ah! wretch - ed, wretch-ed Is - ra - el!
A
p
fall'n how low,
fall'n how low,
mp
from joy - ous
fall'n how low,
mp
from joy - ous
fall'n how low,
mp
from joy - ous
pp
p
pp
mp

from joy - ous trans-port to_ de-sponding
trans-port, from joy - ous trans-port to de-sponding
trans-port, from joy - ous trans-port to_ de-sponding
trans-port, from joy - ous trans-port to de-sponding
woe; wretch-ed Is - ra - el! wretch-ed, wretch - ed! fall'n,
woe; wretch-ed Is - rael! wretch-ed, wretch - ed! fall'n,
woe; wretch-ed Is - rael! wretch - - ed! fall'n,
woe; wretch-ed Is - ra - el! wretch-ed, wretch - ed! fall'n,
fall'n from joy - ous trans - port to de - spond - - ing
fall'n from joy - ous trans - port to de - spond - - ing
fall'n from joy - ous trans - port to de - spond - - ing
fall'n from joy - ous trans - port to de - spond - - ing
mf
p
mp
cresc.
f

B
cresc.
woe; wretch - ed Is - ra - el! fall'n how low, from joy - ous
woe; wretch - ed Is - ra - el! fall'n how low, from joy - ous
woe; wretch - ed Is - ra - el! fall'n how low, from joy - ous
woe; wretch - ed Is - ra - el! fall'n how low,
trans-port to de-spond-ing woe; wretch-ed Is - ra - el! fall'n how
trans-port to de-spond-ing woe; from joy - ous trans-port to de-spond-ing
trans-port to de-spond-ing woe; wretch-ed
from joy - ous trans-port to de-spond-ing
low, from joy - ous trans-port to de-spond-ing woe,
woe, wretch-ed Is - ra - el! ah! wretch - ed
Is - ra - el! fall'n how low! ah! wretch - ed
woe, wretch-ed Is - ra - el! wretch-ed
dim.
mf
mp

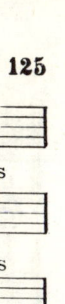

C
fall'n how low,
Is-ra-el! fall'n how low,
Is-ra-el! fall'n how low, fall'n how
Is-ra-el! fall'n how low, fall'n how
from joy-ous trans-port, from joy-ous
from joy-ous trans port, from joy-ous
low, from joy-ous trans-port, from joy-ous
low, from joy-ous trans-port, from joy-ous
trans-port to de-spond-ing woe, fall'n how low, from joy-ous
trans-port to de-spond-ing woe, fall'n how low, from joy-ous
trans-port to de-spond-ing woe, fall'n how low, from joy-ous
trans-port to de-spond-ing woe, fall'n how low, from joy-ous

127

Nº 27. RECIT.—"My arms!"

JUDAS MACCABAEUS

My arms! a-gainst this Gor-gias will I go! The I-du-me-an gov-ern-or shall know How vain, how in-ef-fect-ive his de-sign, While rage his lead-er, and Je-ho-vah mine.

№ 28. AIR AND CHORUS.—"Sound an alarm!"

JUDAS MACCABAEUS
Allegro marziale

Sound an a-larm, sound an a-larm! your sil-ver trumpets sound, And call the brave, and on-ly brave, and on-ly brave, a-round, call the brave, call the brave, and on-ly brave, a-round!

Sound an a-larm! your sil-ver trum-pets sound, your trum-pets sound, your trum-pets sound, And call the brave, and on-ly brave, and call the brave, and on-ly brave, and on-ly brave, a-round, call the brave, call the brave,

cresc.
and on - ly brave, a -
cresc.
round!
A
Who list - eth, fol - low: to the field a - gain!
Jus - tice, with cour - age, is a thou - sand men, is a thou - sand
cresc.
men, jus - tice, with cour - age, jus - tice, with cour - age, is a thou - sand men, is a
cresc.

thou-sand men, is a thou-sand men. Sound an a-larm! Sound an a-larm, your sil-ver trumpets sound! And call the brave, and on-ly brave, and on-ly brave, a-round! Sound an a-larm! your sil-ver trum-pets sound, And call the brave, and on-ly brave, and on-ly brave, a-round!

a piacere
a tempo
più largo
a tempo

134

cresc.
and fol-low thee, and fol - low thee to con-quest:
If to fall, if to fall, For
cresc.
pp
laws, re - li-gion, lib - er - ty, we fall! We
mf
f
ff

136

fall, For laws, re-li-gion, for lib-er-ty, we
fall, For laws, re-li-gion, for lib-er-ty, we
fall, For laws, re-li-gion, for lib-er-ty, we
fall, For laws, re-li-gion, for lib-er-ty, we

fall, for laws, re-li-gion, for lib-er-ty, we
fall, for laws, re-li-gion, for lib-er-ty, we
fall, for laws, re-li-gion, for lib-er-ty, we
fall, for laws, re-li-gion, for lib-er-ty, we

fall.
fall.
fall.
fall.

*Optional version in small type

N⁰ 29. RECIT.—"Enough! To Heav'n we leave the rest"

SIMON

E-nough! To Heav'n we leave the rest! Such gen-'rous ar-dour fir-ing ev-'ry breast, We may di-vide our cares; the field be thine, Oh Ju-das, and the sanc-tu-a-ry mine; For Si-on, ho-ly Si-on, seat of God, In ruin-ous heaps, is by the hea-then trod. Down, down with the pol-lut-ed al-tars, down! Hurl Ju-pi-ter O-lym-pius from his throne, Nor rev-e-rence Bac-chus with his i-vy crown! Our fa-thers nev-er knew him

or his hat-ed crew, Or, know-ing, scorn'd such i-dol van-i-ties.

attacca Nº 30

Nº 30. CHORUS. "We never will bow down"

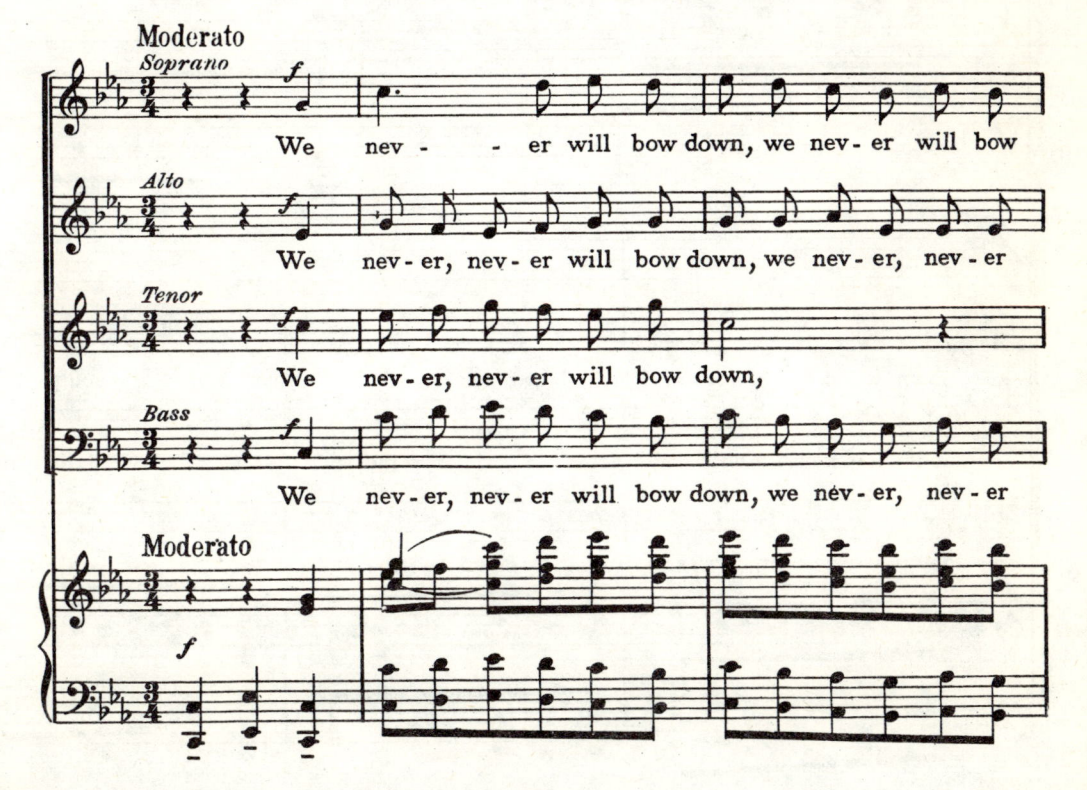

Moderato

Soprano
We nev - - er will bow down, we nev-er will bow

Alto
We nev-er, nev-er will bow down, we nev-er, nev-er

Tenor
We nev-er, nev-er will bow down,

Bass
We nev-er, nev-er will bow down, we nev-er, nev-er

down To the rude stock or sculp-tur'd stone, to the rude
will bow down To the rude stock or sculp-tur'd stone, to the rude
nev-er, To the rude stock or sculp-tur'd stone, to the rude
will bow down To the rude stock or sculp-tur'd stone, to the rude
stock or sculp-tur'd stone,
stock or sculp-tur'd stone, we nev-er, nev-er will bow
stock or sculp-tur'd stone, we nev-er will bow
stock or sculp-tur'd stone, we nev-er will bow
down, we nev-er, nev-er will bow down to the rude stock or sculp-tur'd
down, we nev-er will bow down to the rude stock or sculp-tur'd
down, we nev-er, nev-er will bow down to the rude stock or sculp-tur'd

141

142

never, never will bow down, we never, never will bow down to the rude stock or sculptur'd stone, sculptur'd stone, we never, never will bow down to the rude stock, stock or sculptur'd, sculptur'd stone; we to the rude stock or sculptur'd stone; we down to the rude stock, we never, never will bow we never, never will bow never, never will bow down, we never, never will bow never, never will bow down, we never will bow down, we never, never will bow down, never will bow down, we never, never will bow down

144

145

-ship God, we worship God, and God alone, and God alone, we worship God alone, and God alone, we worship God, we worship God alone, and God alone, we worship God, and God alone, we worship God alone, we worship God alone, we worship God, we worship God alone,

147

-ship God, and God a-lone, and God a-lone, we wor-ship
lone, and God a-lone, and God a-lone, we wor-ship
and God a-lone, and God a-lone, we wor-ship
lone, and God a-lone, and God a-lone, we wor-ship

God, and God a-lone, and God a-lone, we wor-ship God, we
God, and God a-lone, and God a-lone, we wor-ship
God, and God a-lone, and God a-lone,
God, and God a-lone, and God a-lone, we wor-ship

149

Part III

N⁰ 31. AIR.— "Father of Heav'n!"

Andante larghetto

PRIEST (Alto) ad lib.
Fa - ther of Heav'n!   Fa - ther of Heav'n! from Thy e-ter-nal throne, from Thy e-ter-nal throne   Look with an eye   of

bless-ing down, While we pre-pare, with ho-ly rites, To sol-em-nize the Feast of Lights. Fa-ther of Heav'n! from Thy e-ter-nal throne Look with an eye of bless-ing down, While we pre-pare, with ho-ly rites, To sol-em-nize the Feast of Lights, the Feast of Lights, to sol-em-nize the Feast of Lights, while we pre-pare, with ho-ly rites, to sol-em-nize the Feast of Lights,

And thus our

153

grate - ful hearts em - ploy, And in Thy praise This al-tar raise With car-ols of tri-umph-ant joy,— this al-tar raise with car-ols of tri - umph - ant joy,—

Ossia — with car-ols of tri - umph - ant joy.— Fa-ther of Heav'n!

20750

154

from Thy e-ter-nal throne, from Thy e-ter-nal throne

Look with an eye of bless-ing down, While we pre-pare,

— with ho-ly rites, To sol-em-nize the Feast of Lights, the Feast of

Lights, to sol-em-nize the Feast of Lights.

20750

№ 32. RECIT.—"Oh grant it, Heav'n"

ISRAELITISH WOMAN (*Soprano*)

Oh grant it, Heav'n, that our long woes may cease, And Judah's daughters taste the calm of peace; Sons, brothers, husbands to bewail no more, Tortur'd at home, or havock'd in the war.

attacca № 33

Nº 33. AIR.— "So shall the lute and harp awake"

ISRAELITISH WOMAN (Soprano)

So shall the lute and harp a-wake, And spright-ly voice sweet des-cant run, so shall the lute a-wake, so shall the harp a-wake, so shall the lute and harp a-wake, and spright-ly voice sweet des-cant run, and spright - ly voice sweet des - cant run, and spright - - - - - - ly voice sweet des - cant run,_____ and spright - - - - - -

-ly voice sweet des-cant run,

Se-raph-ic mel-o-dy to make, In the pure strains of Jes-se's son, se-raph- -ic mel-o-dy to make In the pure strains, in

the pure strains of Jes - se's son,
f
p
se-
raph-ic mel-o - dy to make
pp
p
in the pure strains of
poco rit.
a tempo
mp
Jes - se's son, in the pure strains,
a tempo
poco rit.
cresc.
mf
in the pure strains of
mp

Jes - se's son.

So shall the lute a-wake, so shall the harp a-wake, so shall the lute and harp a-wake, and spright-ly voice sweet descant run, and spright-ly voice sweet des-cant run, and spright -

161

No. 34. RECIT.—"From Capharsalama on eagle wings I fly"

ISRAELITISH MESSENGER

From Ca-phar-sa-la-ma on ea-gle wings I fly, With ti-dings of im-pet-uous joy: Came Ly-si-as, with his host, ar-ray'd In coat of mail; their mas-sy shields Of gold and brass, flash'd light-ning o'er the fields; But Ju-das, un-dis-may'd, Met, fought, and van-quish'd all the rage-ful train.

But lo! the con-quer-or comes; and on his spear, To dis-si-pate all fear, He bears the vaunt-er's head and hand, That threaten'd des-o-la-tion to the land.

Attacca Nº 35

Nº 35. CHORUS.— "See, the conqu'ring hero comes!"

YOUTHS

Soprano I
See, the con-qu'ring he-ro comes! Sound the

Soprano II
See, the con-qu'ring he-ro comes! Sound the

Alto
See, the con-qu'ring he-ro comes! Sound the

★ If a children's choir is not available, the part of *Youths* is sung by the ladies of the chorus, and the part of *Virgins* by the Soloists (Soprano and Alto)
20750

trum-pets, beat the drums.

trum-pets, beat the drums.

trum-pets, beat the drums.

Sports prepare, the laurels

Sports prepare, the laurels

Sports prepare, the laurels

bring, Songs of triumph to him sing, Sports pre-

bring, Songs of triumph to him sing, Sports pre-

bring, Songs of triumph to him sing, Sports pre-

165

pare, the lau - rels bring, Songs of tri-umph to him sing.

pare, the lau - rels bring, Songs of tri-umph to him sing.

pare, the lau - rels bring, Songs of tri-umph to him sing.

CHORUS

VIRGINS
Sop. I.
See the god-like youth advance! Breathe the

Sop. II.
See the god-like youth advance! Breathe the

flutes, and lead the dance; Myr - tle-wreaths and

flutes, and lead the dance; Myr - tle-wreaths and

20750

roses twine, To deck the hero's brow divine; Myrtle wreaths and roses twine, To deck the hero's brow divine.

167

(Children's Choir, with Sopranos and Altos)

FULL CHORUS

Soprano: See, the con-qu'ring he - ro comes! Sound the trum-pets,
Alto: See, the con-qu'ring he - ro comes! Sound the trum-pets,
Tenor: See, the con-qu'ring he - ro comes! Sound the trum-pets,
Bass: See, the con-qu'ring he - ro comes! Sound the trum-pets,

(Without Children's Choir)

beat the drums. Sports pre-pare, the lau-rels bring,
beat the drums. Sports pre-pare, the lau-rels bring,
beat the drums. Sports pre-pare, the lau-rels bring,
beat the drums. Sports pre-pare, the lau-rels bring,

20750

(With Children's Choir)
cresc.
ff
Songs of triumph to him sing. See, the
conqu'ring he - ro comes! Sound the trumpets, beat the drums.
rit.
Attacca No 36

№ 36. MARCH

Allegro

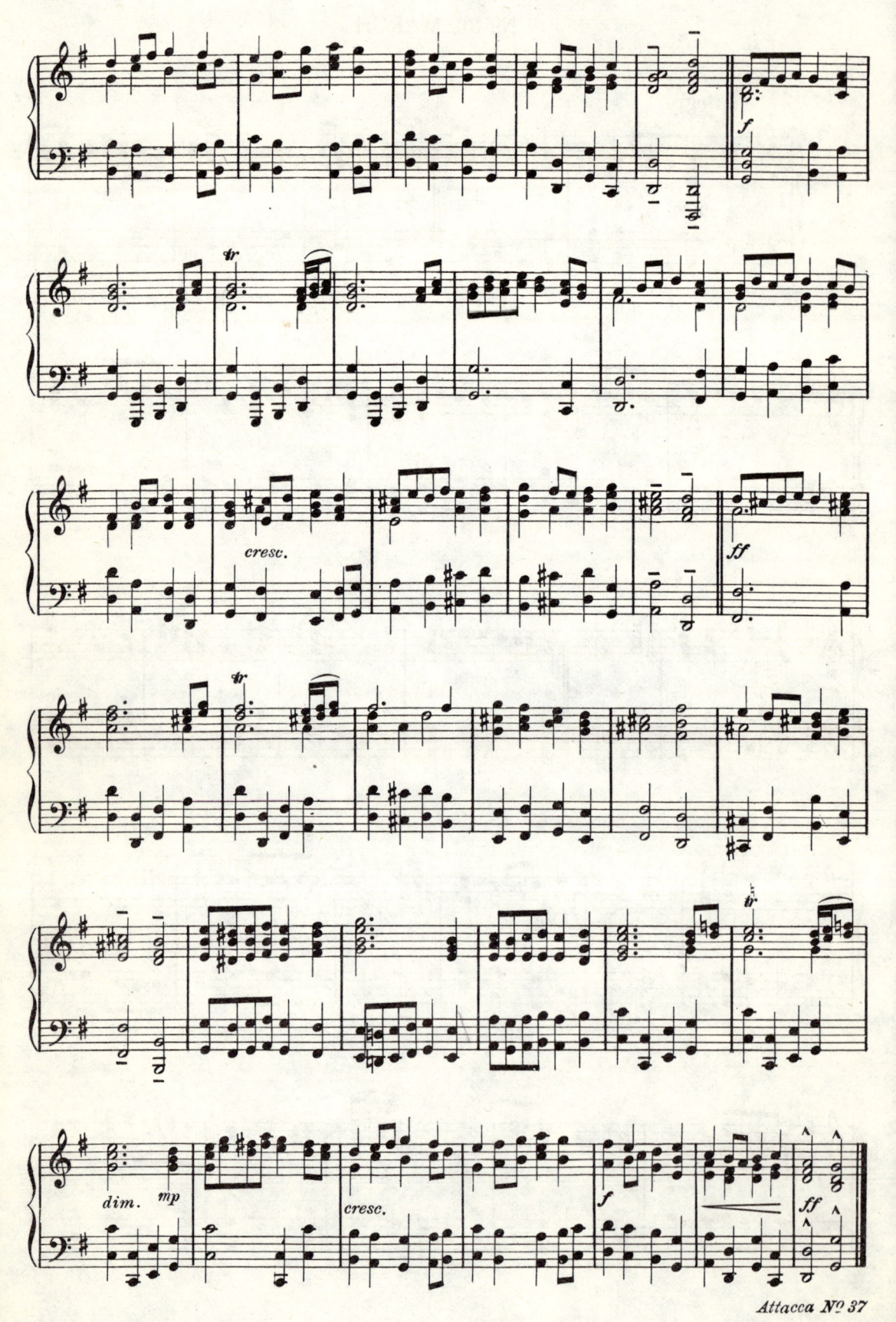

Attacca No. 37

Nº 37. CHORUS.—"Sing unto God"

Allegro maestoso

Sing un-to God, and high af-fec-tions raise, To crown this conquest with

★ The three introductory measures in smaller type are an optional addition connecting the Chorus with the preceding March

un-mea-sur'd praise, with un-mea-sur'd praise. Sing un-to God, and high af-fec-tions raise, To crown this con-quest with un-mea-sur'd praise,

with un-mea-sur'd praise. Sing un-to God, and
Sing un-to God, and
Sing un-to God, and
Sing un-to God, and

high af-fec-tions raise, To crown this con-quest with un-mea-sur'd praise, with
high af-fec-tions raise, To crown this con-quest with un-mea-sur'd praise,
high af-fec-tions raise, To crown this con-quest with un-mea-sur'd praise, with
high af-fec-tions raise, To crown this con-quest with un-mea-sur'd praise,

praise, with praise, with un-mea-sur'd praise,
with praise, with un-mea-sur'd praise,
praise, with praise, with un-mea-sur'd praise, with
with

un-mea-sur'd praise, to
un-mea-sur'd praise, with un-mea-sur'd praise.

f
sing un - to God, and high af - fec - tions raise, to
mf
to crown, to crown, to
crown, to crown this con-quest, to
mf
crown this con-quest with un-mea - sur'd praise,
crown this con-quest, to crown this con-quest with
mp
crown this con-quest, this
mp
cresc.
f
with un-
un - mea - sur'd praise, to crown this con-quest with un-
cresc.
con-quest, to crown this con-quest
cresc.

175

to crown this con-quest with
crown this con-quest, to crown, to crown this con-quest with un-
to crown, to crown, to crown this con-quest
un-mea - sur'd praise, to crown this con-quest with un-mea-sur'd,

un-mea - sur'd praise,
mea - sur'd praise, to crown, to crown, to crown
with un-mea-sur'd praise, to crown
with un-mea-sur'd praise, to crown, to crown, to

to crown this con-quest, this con-quest
this con-quest, this con-quest
this con-quest, this con-quest
crown, to crown this con-quest, this con-quest

with un-mea-sur'd praise; Sing un-to God, sing un-to God, and
with un-mea-sur'd praise; Sing un-to God, sing un-to God, and
with un-mea-sur'd praise; Sing un-to God, sing un-to God, and
with un-mea-sur'd praise; Sing un-to God, sing un-to God, and

★ Optional version in small type

20750

high af - fec - tions raise, and high af - fec-tions raise, To crown,
high af - fec - tions raise, and high af - fec - tions raise, To
high af - fec - tions raise, and high af - fec - tions raise, To
high af - fec - tions raise, and high af - fec-tions raise, To
to crown, to crown, to crown this con-quest
crown, to crown, to crown this con-quest with
crown, to crown, to__ crown, to crown this con-quest
crown, to crown, to crown this con-quest with
with un-mea-sur'd praise,
un-mea - - sur'd praise,
with un-mea-sur'd praise, to crown this con - quest
un-mea - - sur'd praise, to crown this con - quest
f
mf
mp
cresc.

to crown this conquest with unmeasur'd praise, to crown this conquest with unmeasur'd praise, to crown this conquest with unmeasur'd praise, this conquest with unmeasur'd praise.

with unmeasur'd praise, to crown this conquest with unmeasur'd
with unmeasur'd praise, to crown

Più largo

praise, this conquest with unmea - sur'd praise.
praise, this conquest with un - mea - sur'd praise.
praise, this conquest with un - mea - sur'd praise.
this conquest with un - mea - sur'd praise.

No. 38. RECIT. — "Sweet flow the strains"

JUDAS MACCABAEUS
Cantabile

Sweet flow the strains that strike my feast-ed ear; An-gels might stoop from Heav'n to hear The come-ly songs ye sing To Is-rael's Lord and King.

No. 39. AIR. — "No unhallowed desire"

Allegro marcato

No, no un-hal-low'd de-sire Our breasts shall in-spire,

no, Nor lust of un-bounded pow'r, nor lust of un-bound-ed pow'r! No, no un-hal-low'd de-sire Our breasts shall in-spire, Nor lust of un-bound-ed pow'r, nor lust of un-bound-ed pow'r, nor lust of un-bound-ed pow'r! But peace to ob-tain, Free peace let us gain, And con-quest shall

ask no more,___ no more, no more, and

con-quest shall ask no more;

But peace t'ob-tain, Free peace let us gain,___ And con-quest shall ask no

mp
f
mf
more, and con-quest shall ask no more, no more, no
f
p
mf
mp
more, no more,
cresc.
p
cresc.
f
mf
and conquest shall ask no more, But peace to ob-
mf
mp
f
rit.
tain, Free peace let us gain, And con-quest shall ask no
mf
f rit.
mf
a tempo
more!
a tempo
f

No. 40. DUET.— "Oh lovely peace"

Allegro moderato

love-ly peace, with plen-ty crown'd, oh love-ly, love-ly peace! Come, spread

185

hills a-dorn,_____ And val-leys smile with wav-y corn;

hills a-dorn,_____ And val-leys smile with wav-y corn;

Let fleec-y flocks the hills a-dorn. And

And val-leys smile with wav-y corn, and

val-leys smile_____ with wav-y corn, and smile_____

val-leys smile_____ with wav-y corn, and

_____ with wav - y corn, with wav - y corn,

smile_____ with wav - y corn, with

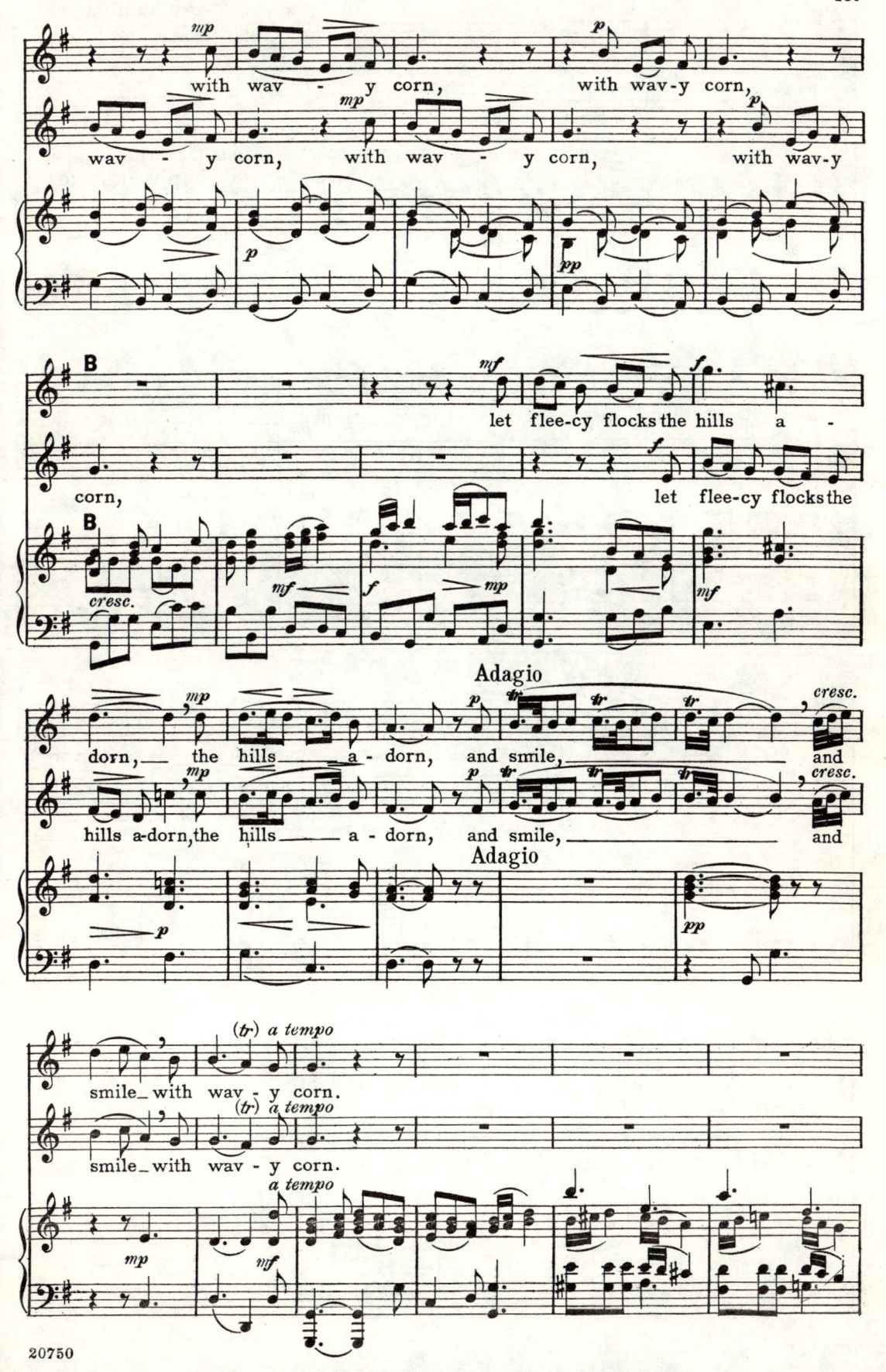

with wavy corn, with wavy corn, wavy corn, with wavy corn, with wavy

let fleecy flocks the hills adorn, let fleecy flocks the

dorn, the hills adorn, and smile, and hills adorn, the hills adorn, and smile, and

smile with wavy corn.
smile with wavy corn.

Poco più animato
Let the shrill trum-pet
Poco più animato
cresc.
Let the shrill trum-pet cease, nor oth-er sound But na-ture's
cease, nor oth-er sound
song - sters wake the cheer - ful morn, nor oth - er sound, nor
But na-ture's song - sters wake the
oth - er sound wake cheer - ful morn, but na - ture's songsters wake the
cheer - ful morn, the cheer - ful morn, but na - ture's songsters wake the

C
cheer - ful morn, nor oth - er
mp
cheer - ful morn, nor oth - er sound
C
sound but na-ture's song - - - - - sters, na-ture's
but na-ture's song - - - - - sters, na-ture's
(tr)
song - sters wake the cheerful morn, but na-ture's song-sters wake the
cresc.
song - sters wake the cheerful morn, but na - ture's
cresc.
rit.
a tempo I
cheer - - - ful, wake the cheer - ful morn. Oh
song-sters wake the cheer - ful, the cheer - ful morn.
a tempo I
rit.
mp

mf
mp
love-ly peace, with plen-ty crown'd, oh love-ly, love-ly peace! Come, spread
thy_ bless-ings, thy_ bless-ings all_ a-round. Let
Let
fleec-y flocks the hills a-dorn,_ And val-leys smile with
fleec-y flocks the hills a-dorn,_ And val-leys smile with
wav-y corn, let fleec-y flocks the hills a-dorn,
wav-y corn, and
p
mp

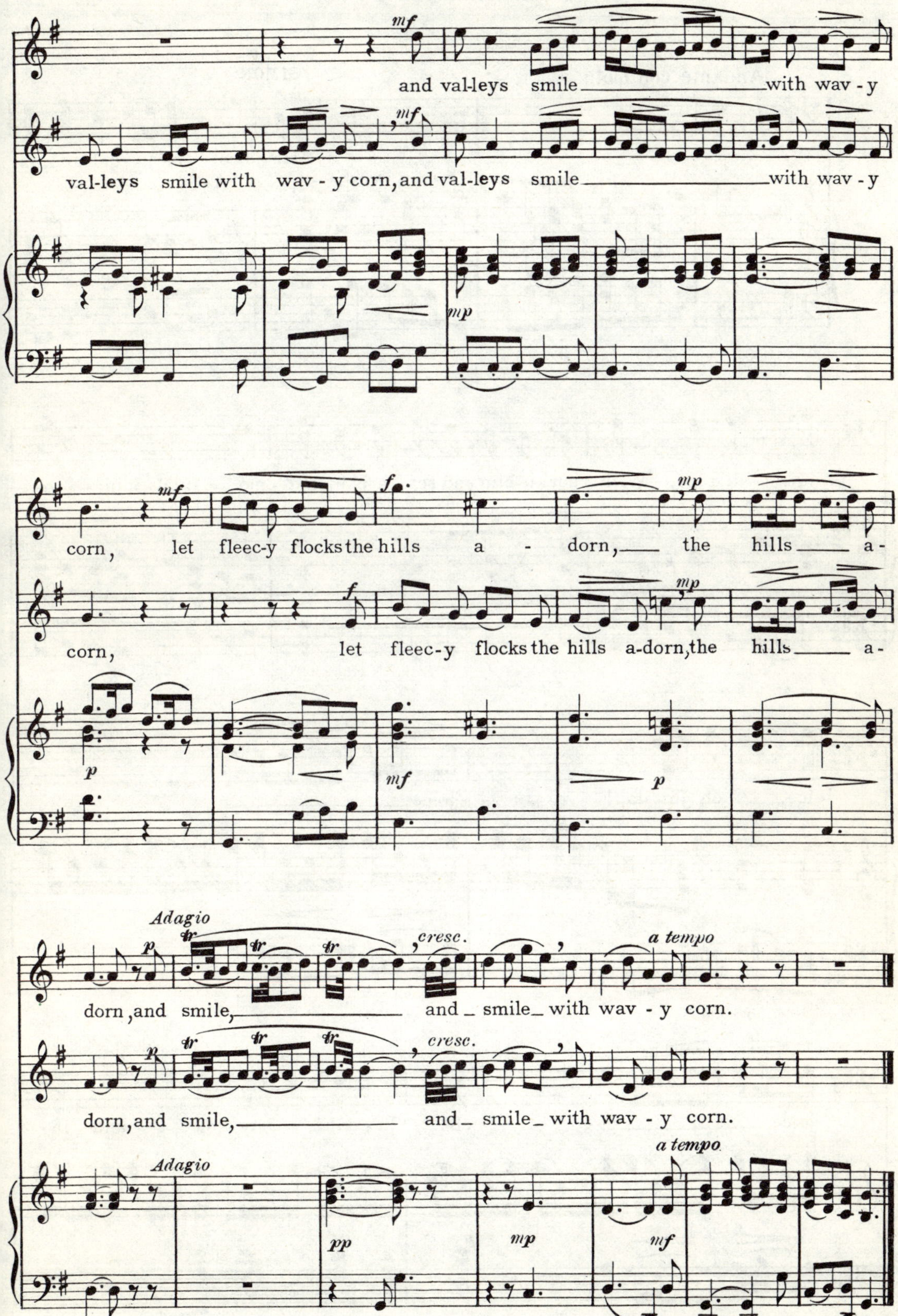
mf
and val-leys smile with wav - y
mf
val-leys smile with wav - y corn, and val-leys smile with wav - y
mp
mf
f
mp
corn, let flee-y flocks the hills a - dorn, the hills a-
f
mp
corn, let fleec-y flocks the hills a-dorn, the hills a-
p
mf
p
Adagio
p
cresc.
a tempo
dorn, and smile, and smile with wav - y corn.
p
cresc.
dorn, and smile, and smile with wav - y corn.
Adagio
a tempo
pp
mp
mf

No. 41. AIR AND CHORUS.—"Rejoice, oh Judah!"

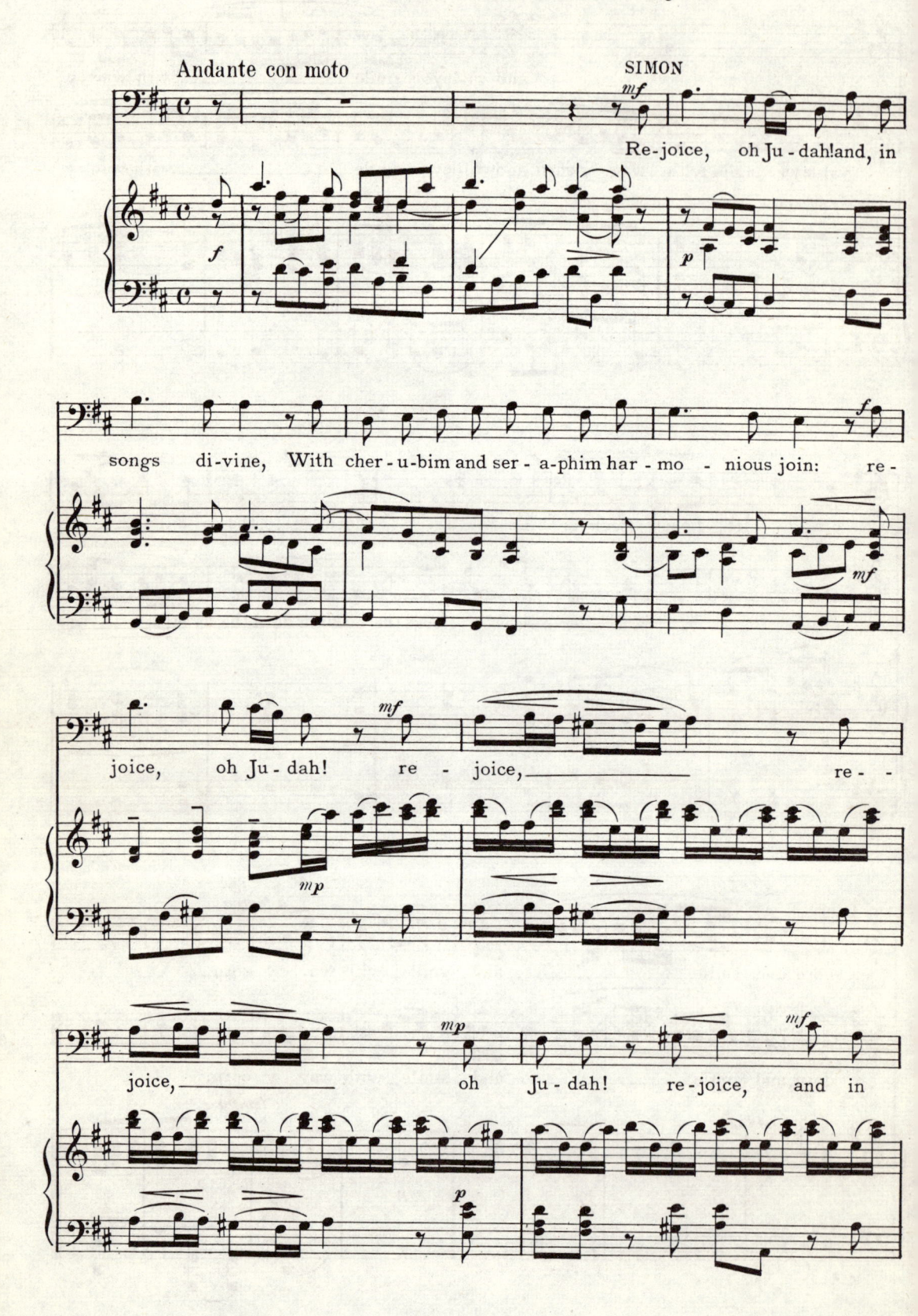

Andante con moto

SIMON

Rejoice, oh Judah! and, in songs divine, With cherubim and seraphim harmonious join: rejoice, oh Judah! rejoice, rejoice, oh Judah! rejoice, and in

songs di-vine, with cher-u-bim and ser-a-phim har-
mo-nious join, and in songs di-vine har-
mo-nious join; re-joice, oh Ju-dah! re-
joice, oh Ju-dah! re-joice, re-
mp
p
mf
A
f

joice! Witn cher - u-bim and ser - a-phim
har - mo - - nious
join in songs di - vine, with
cresc.
cher - u-bim and ser - a-phim har-mo - nious, har-mo - nious join.

Allegro, a tempo giusto

CHILDREN'S CHOIR ★

Hal-le-lu-jah, a-men,

Soprano

Alto

Hal-le-lu-jah, a-men,

Tenor

Hal-le-lu-jah, a-men,

Bass

Hal-le-lu-jah, a-men, a-men, hal-le-lu-jah, a-men.

Allegro, a tempo giusto

★ If a Children's choir is not available, the chorus sings the original version in small type

a-men, hal-le-lu - jah, a - men.
Hal - le - lu - jah, a-men, a-men, hal-le - lu - jah, a -
a-men, hal-le-lu - jah, a - men. Hal-le-lu - jah, hal-le-lu - jah, hal - le-
a-men, hal-le-lu - jah, a - men. Hal-le-lu-jah, a-men, a-men, hal - le - lu-
Hal - le - lu - jah, a-men, a-men, hal-le - lu - jah, hal -
men, a - - men, a - men, hal - le - lu - jah, hal -
-lu - jah, hal - le - lu - jah, hal - le - lu - jah,
jah, hal - le - lu - jah, hal - le - lu - jah,
-le - lu - jah, hal - le - lu-jah,

Children's Choir
Soprano f
Hal - le - - - lu - jah!
Alto f
Hal -
-le - lu - jah, hal - le - - - lu - jah! Hal-le - lu - jah, a-men,
hal - le - lu - jah, a-men, a-men, hal-le - lu - jah, a - men.
hal - le - lu - jah!
Hal - le - lu - jah, a-men,
hal - le - lu - jah, a-men, a-men, hal-le - lu - jah, a - men.
B
-le - - - lu - jah!
a-men, hal-le - lu - jah, a - men. Oh Ju - dah, re-joice, re - joice,
Oh Ju - dah, re-joice, re - joice,
a-men, hal-le - lu - jah, a - men. Oh Ju - dah, re-joice, re - joice,
Oh Ju - dah, re-joice, re - joice,
ff

rejoice, oh Judah, in songs di-
rejoice, oh Judah, in songs di-
rejoice, oh Judah, in songs di-
rejoice, oh Judah, in songs di-

CHILDREN (*Soprano*)
Hal - le - lu -
vine, with cherubim and seraphim harmonious
vine, with cherubim and seraphim harmonious
vine, with cherubim and seraphim harmonious
vine,

(Alto) pp
jah! Hal - le - lu -
join, with cher-u-bim and ser-a-phim har-mo - nious
join, with cher-u-bim and ser-a-phim har-mo - nious
join, with cher-u-bim and ser-a-phim har-mo - nious
p
With cher - u-bim and ser-a-phim har-mo - nious
jah!
mf
join. Hal-le-lu-jah, a-men, a-men, hal-le-lu-jah, a -
mf
join, har - mo - nious join. Hal - le - lu -
mf
join. Hal-le-lu-jah, a-men, a-men, hal-le-lu-jah, a -
mf
join, har - mo - - - - nious
mf

cresc.
men, and, in songs di - -
cresc.
jah! and, in songs di - -
cresc.
men, and, in songs di - -
cresc.
join, and, in songs di - -
cresc.
f
vine, har - mo - nious join! Hal - le - lu - jah, a - men,
f
ff
vine, har - mo - nious join! Hal - le - lu - jah, a - men,
f
ff
vine, har - mo - nious join! Hal - le - lu - jah, a - men,
f
ff
vine, har - mo - nious join! Hal - le - lu - jah, a - men,
f
ff
f
ff

ff
Hal - le - lu - jah!
a-men, hal - le - lu - jah, a - men. A -
a-men, hal - le - lu - jah, a - men. A -
a-men, hal - le - lu - jah, a - men. A -
a-men, hal - le - lu - jah, a - men. A -
Molto maestoso
fff
Hal - le - lu - jah! Hal - le - lu-jah! A - men.
men. A-men. Hal - le - lu-jah! A - men.
men. A-men. Hal - le - lu-jah! A - men.
men. A-men. Hal - le - lu-jah! A - men.
men. A-men. Hal - le - lu-jah! A - men.
Molto maestoso

Dec 9   long skirt white blouse
Dec 11